RESILIENCY & OVERCOMING TRAUMA

How to Thrive and
not just Survive

ROBERT L. BOWERS

Copyright © 2024 by Robert L. Bowers

All rights reserved. No part of this book may be used or reproduced in any manner whatsoever without prior written consent of the author, except as provided by the United States of America copyright law.

Published by Best Seller Publishing®, St. Augustine, FL
Best Seller Publishing® is a registered trademark.
Printed in the United States of America.

ISBN: 978-1-966395-81-2

This publication is designed to provide accurate and authoritative information with regard to the subject matter covered. It is sold with the understanding that the publisher is not engaged in rendering legal, accounting, or other professional advice. If legal advice or other expert assistance is required, the services of a competent professional should be sought. The opinions expressed by the author in this book are not endorsed by Best Seller Publishing® and are the sole responsibility of the author rendering the opinion.

For more information, please write:
Best Seller Publishing®
1775 US-1 #1070
St. Augustine, FL 32084
or call 1 (626) 765-9750
Visit us online at: www.BestSellerPublishing.org

RESILIENCY & OVERCOMING TRAUMA

Table of Contents

Introduction 1

1. The Aftermath and Trauma 5
2. Learn from Your Past 15
3. Post Trauma Impacts & Coping Methods 23
4. Eight Years Was Long Enough 31
5. The Illusion of Closure 41
6. The Unthinkable — Is This a Bad Dream? 49
7. My Old Friend "Pain" 59
8. A Rehabilitation in the Gym & Life 69
9. Mothers Gifts & Finding Purpose 79
10. Broken Heart 91
11. Final Thoughts & Lessons Learned 107
May Chapter 12 Never Come! 117

Afterword 119

Dedication

Dedicated to mom for fulfilling a promise,
Holly for going through every minute of trauma with me,
Derek and Kayln for being there over and
over with your love, and for those whose
life is interrupted by Trauma/Loss.

C. TODD SHERMAN

Law enforcement and emergency personnel work the scene of an hit-and-run accident Wednesday on the Natchez Trace at Cliff Gookin Boulevard. A bicyclist was struck by a vehicle and suffered serious injuries. Authorities are looking for a dark burgundy Ford F-150 in connection with the incident.

HIT-AND-RUN

Cyclist injured in Trace accident

■ The victim suffered serious injuries after apparently being hit by a truck.

BY DANZA JOHNSON
Daily Journal

TUPELO — Natchez Trace Parkway officials are looking for a vehicle involved in a Wednesday afternoon hit-and-run that left a cyclist injured.

About 1:25 p.m. on the Natchez Trace near Cliff Gookin Boulevard, a person was hit while riding a bicycle just south of Tupelo High School. According to authorities, the victim's injuries were serious but not life-threatening. The victim's name was not released.

Authorities are looking for a dark burgundy Ford F-150 in connection with the hit and run. Police said the truck should have considerable front-end damage as well as damage to the passenger side door.

This is the first bicycle accident on the Trace since two fatalities in 2009.

Anyone with information about Wednesday's incident should call 911.

Contact **Danza Johnson** at (662) 678-1583 or danza.johnson@djournal.com.

Introduction

December 22, 2010.

As my eyes fluttered open, I found myself lying on my side amidst a sea of grass. I could feel the sun's warm embrace casting a gentle glow over my body. There was an incredible sense of serenity, a profound peacefulness enveloping me as I lay there. I could feel the soft blades of grass on my cheek, and as I swallowed, I became acutely aware of an unprecedented tranquility. The warmth of the sun felt as though it was directed solely at me. As my surroundings slowly came into focus, I remembered that I had been on a bike ride. It was December 22, 2010. I had been cycling along the Natchez Trace near Tupelo, Mississippi. Reality started to set in—I must have been in an accident.

My first instinct was to assess the damage inflicted upon my body. Cautiously, I attempted to move my arms, quickly realizing that my right shoulder was injured, possibly broken. As I tried to move my legs, a sharp pain surged from my hip down through my knees and ankle. As I tried to roll over on my back, pain radiated up my entire spine. This was far from the idyllic Christmas break I had envisioned at my parents' home.

Soon, a voice broke through the silence, drawing nearer. Someone was asking if I was okay. They had called an ambulance and stayed by my side, offering comfort while we waited. During this time, I managed to give them my parents' phone number. They called my family, who arrived at the scene just as the ambulance did. My memories remain sketchy concerning the medical personnel attending to me and loading me in the ambulance. I do remember being in the ambulance, the siren blaring, uncertain of the extent of my injuries or how things would unfold. Later, I learned I had been involved in a hit-and-run. A pickup truck had struck me from behind, and I landed roughly 35 feet from the point of impact. A young girl who witnessed the accident recounted that my body and bike were thrown through the air, tumbling until they crashed into the grass. She was outside her vehicle, in tears, when another vehicle stopped, to offer assistance. She told the driver she had witnessed a man being hit and killed. It took some time for him to understand her, but eventually, she directed him to where I lay, entangled with my bicycle.

In the aftermath of the accident, my body was severely battered. I was fortunate to be alive. My injuries included a broken collarbone, severe head trauma, multiple spinal compression fractures and soft tissue damage throughout my body. Little did I know that the impact of this day would resonate throughout my future. The mental, emotional and physical pain would become a constant companion in my life.

This was the day the seed of resilience was planted in my mind.

This accident tested me on multiple levels. Emotionally, the reality of potentially facing death was hard to grasp. I couldn't comprehend how a human being could injure another in such a manner without attending to them. The shock of surviving such an impact was also met with confusion mentally. How was I still here? Physically, the pain throughout my body made every waking moment unbearable. This traumatic event would challenge me mentally and physically more than I had ever been challenged before. I had no idea the trauma would last for years. At the time I couldn't see past my two primary motivations to recover as quickly as possible. First, I was in my first year as a high school principal. It was crucial for me to return and continue building relationships and providing leadership. Second, I was determined to get back on my bicycle and reintegrate cycling as a part of my weekly routine. My life was built around fitness being an important aspect of my daily life mentally and physically.

1
The Aftermath and Trauma

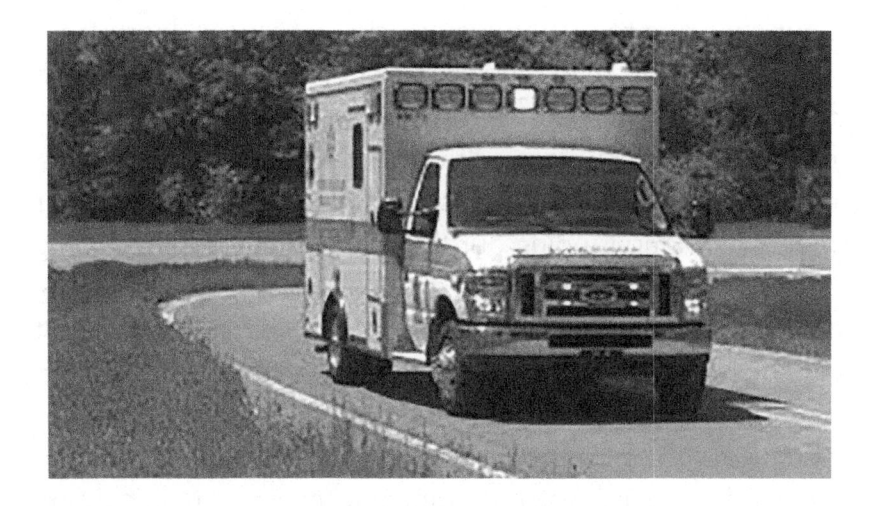

As a child, it was a sunny afternoon, and I was racing down our neighborhood street when I hit a large hole in the sidewalk and went flying over the handlebars. The impact was jarring, leaving me with scraped knees and a bruised ego. Yet, amid my tears and the sting of cleaning my wounds, I never gave a second thought to whether I would get back on the bicycle. Soon I was back to racing down the street, embracing the freedom that cycling brought me. I never imagined decades later I would be revisiting some of my childhood experiences, trying to understand resilience and the key role it plays in our lives.

Resilience is not just about weathering the storm but learning to dance in the rain. It is the ability to bounce back from adversity, recover from setbacks and keep going in the face of hardship. It is a quality that allows us to navigate through life's traumas, not just to survive, but to thrive. A life of resilience is not one devoid of hardship, but one that embraces challenges as opportunities for growth. It is about understanding that life is not always fair, that pain is part of human experience and that it is our response to these trials that defines us. It is about choosing to rise above our circumstances, learn from our mistakes and keep moving forward, no matter how tough the journey may be. Resilience is not a trait that we are born with but a skill that we can cultivate. It requires self-awareness, self-care and a positive mindset. It involves recognizing our emotions, understanding our triggers and developing coping strategies. It means taking care of our physical health, nurturing our mental wellbeing and fostering our spiritual growth. It demands a positive outlook on life, a belief in our abilities and a commitment to personal growth. A life of resilience is a life of empowerment. It is about taking control, setting a path and shaping destiny. It is about finding purpose, pursuing passion and realizing potential. It is about living life on our own terms, not as victims of our circumstances, but as masters of our fate. In the end, a life of resilience is a life well-lived. It is a life of courage, strength and triumph. It is a life that embraces adversity, learns from failure and celebrates success. It is a life that not only survives but thrives.

The hit and run accident put me on a journey of physical therapy and various treatments for years. I believe my prior experiences somewhat prepared me for this arduous process. As a dedicated athlete, I had actively participated in numerous sports, including baseball, track, cross country and basketball.

My passion for physical activity and sports steered me toward majoring in physical education and minoring in health during my college years. This academic background provided me with a comprehensive understanding of what it takes to help the body repair and heal. This knowledge increased a great deal during my years coaching. Who knew my passion for athletics and coaching would pay off in a totally unexpected way.

Having endured minor injuries in the past, I was familiar with the necessity of taking time off for rehabilitation. In high school, as a distance runner, I got bad shin splints in both legs. Every time I would start to run, there would be a throbbing pain in each shin. The only cure for shin splints at the time was to take a break from running and let each leg heal. Yes, you could ice your legs to find some relief. Sometimes you could use athletic tape and tape your shins to allow you to continue running. But ultimately, once you had full blown shin splints, the only thing you could do was not run and stay off your feet as much as possible. I remember the mental anguish of not practicing and watching my teammates working hard. Mentally it made me feel I was losing ground and needed to return to practice.

The aftermath of my accident in 2010 was exponentially more devastating than anything I had dealt with in my life. I was in and out of consciousness on the way to the hospital. Once I arrived at the hospital, I remember being rolled to get an MRI done to find out how severe my injuries were. I experienced unimaginable pain when I was lifted off the stretcher and placed on my back on the cold hard surface of the MRI machine. The pain was so severe I felt nauseous, as though I was going to pass out. I was panicking and wanted to escape the pain. In desperation I decided I would distract myself by mentally going back to my high school days and running the 5k cross country course where we ran our races and practiced when I was a high school cross country runner. Distance runners know pain and must be able to handle it to be successful. Running was such a huge part of my life I knew every detail of the course I ran over twenty-five years ago. I still knew every rolling hill, every turn, downhill, steep climbs and each mile mark of the entire course. I put myself mentally on the starting line and set out to run the entire course. My plan was to keep running until my MRI was over and I was off the hard surface which was torturing me mentally and physically. The movement of my body was painful. When the MRI was over It was excruciating to be lifted and put back on the bed. After getting my MRI results it was understandable why the pain was so intense. Being put on a hard surface with a broken collarbone, multiple compression fractures of the spine, severe head trauma and soft tissue damage was unthinkable.

 The shock of what I had been through hit me when I got put in my room at the hospital after the MRI. I was awake and my wife and some family members were in the room. My body started shivering and shaking. I asked for another blanket. One blanket didn't stop the shaking and shivering my entire body was doing. I remember wanting more and more blankets, I just wanted the shaking to stop. The shock and trauma of the accident were revealing themselves during these moments. Eventually the pain medication started to take the edge off the sharp constant pain. I remember interacting with some family members. I was told later my brother-in-law came into the hospital room to see me. I don't remember the interaction but those present never will forget it. He greeted me and I responded, "I wish you had been with me. Maybe they would have hit you." This has been brought up over the years a great many times.

Once it was known my injuries were not going to be life threatening a few days later, I was released from the hospital. I was miserable due to physical pain, and I just wanted to be out of the hospital. This was turning out to be a Christmas unlike any we had before. Over the years my three sisters and our families all gathered at Mom and Dad's for Christmas. Our children grew up with this Christmas tradition. It was the one time during the year the nine nieces and nephews would be together. It was a time of gift exchanges and all our favorite foods. I always looked forward to Christmas because I would be able to enjoy Mom's homemade pumpkin pie, lemon meringue pie and chocolate pie. When I left the hospital, I spent most of my time in bed while back at Mom and Dad's. Christmas activities and what I missed wasn't on my mind. My body still battered and bruised, causing me a great deal of pain and that was dominating every waking moment. I soon learned one of the most natural ways to escape pain is by sleeping. I would rather be asleep during these days because it was the only time I was not in pain. During the days after Christmas my sisters and their families headed home and returned to their post-Christmas lives. I was still spending my time in bed searching for ways to escape pain. I did get help and moved out to the couch after a few days. My goal was to be able to get back to my home in Kentucky and ultimately get better and return to my role as high school principal.

My wife, son and daughter were all handling the shock of the accident in different ways. My wife did an incredible job focusing on my needs and being mentally strong. She wouldn't allow herself to react to anything other than what my needs were as well as our son's and daughter's needs. My son and daughter were both young adults at this point and I could sense their worry and shock from the accident. I could sense relief when I was out of the hospital but the pain and discomfort I was experiencing appeared to be shocking for them. This was the first time my immediate family ever witnessed this type of traumatic event.

After several days of recovery, we made the transition back to my home in Somerset, KY. Riding seven hours in a vehicle was difficult with all the injuries I sustained. I continued to be miserable due to the constant pain. Being back in Somerset didn't make me feel any better physically but I was glad to see my familiar primary care physician and my physical therapist. I felt trust and comfort with them, partially because both were runners. We shared a common passion and understanding concerning distance running. Besides the pain, being gone from my job was my largest concern. Due to the accident, I was away from the school during my first year as principal for a significant amount of time. I fortunately had a young superstar for a vice principal. He would be able to handle things while I was out, but I felt a great deal of guilt, leaving him in a difficult position. Fortunately, I also had a superintendent who was supportive and a friend. One day after work he drove the two hours to Somerset to visit me. He shared the passion of cycling, and we had ridden together from time to time since I took the job. Before his visit was over, he told me we should set a goal to ride in the Tour De Corn, in Missouri which is held late in the Summer. I told him I would be glad to have that as a goal and return to cycling. At this time, it was still painful to move or walk. I was a far cry from being able to ride 65 miles. However, a goal had been set. I was given a reason to focus on rehab. It would be years later before I knew how powerful this small gesture from him was. It was a strategy I could use to focus on rehab and add purpose. Having a purpose keeps you motivated and focused. When confronting a long rehab, it helps to have a specific tangible goal set. This would benefit me, enabling me to focus on this recovery and giving me something to use when faced with future challenges.

It was early February when I eventually returned to work at the high school. I rushed on my return because of the urgency of being a first-year principal at this school and knowing how important it was for me to be there. Getting ready and going to school each day with a broken collarbone and all the other injuries was difficult. One day I remember coming home from school and wanting to lie down on the carpet to relieve my back pain. By being on my feet all day my back was in a great deal of pain as well as my legs, and I just wanted to take the pressure off them. As I sat on the floor and started to lie down on my back, my vertebrae began popping as the weight shifted on my back from my belt line to my neck. This wasn't a good feeling or relief. Each pop was met with sharp, intense pain. The pain was so bad I had tears running down my face. Just the natural weight of my body on my spine was causing an unimaginable amount of pain. The tears were my body's natural response to the pain. Emotionally the pain was excruciating as well. I remember lying on the floor and thinking over and over, "Why did this have to happen to me?" There were multiple times the pain would eventually wear me down and emotionally I would lose it. I was very frustrated because once my sling was gone and my collarbone healed, people would talk to me about how good I looked and how incredible my recovery was. I would always say the right thing, but the truth was underneath my skin my body was still beaten and bruised. Emotionally, the impact of the hit and run had me in worse shape than I thought. I wouldn't see the damage and its extent until years later.

Shortly after my collarbone had healed and I was no longer in a sling, a friend of mine loaned me his recumbent exercise bike. The first time I tried to use it, it was so painful, I could only last a few minutes. I had no idea how much damage was done to my ankle, knee and hamstring on my left leg. As I sat on the bike and started to pedal, each cycle of the pedals was constant pain. Regardless, I was committed to this each day, and slowly but surely each week I got a little bit better. I started to increase the length of my rides, and after about four to six weeks, I was increasing how fast I was riding and pushing myself. This ended up being a great strategy for improving my leg strength and my stamina throughout the day at school. The added benefit of using the recumbent exercise bike was the preparation to get me back into cycling. More important was the regular movement and increased blood flow which aided in healing. Movement is a great treatment for physical and emotional trauma.

After a month or so of riding the exercise bike, I was still searching for pain relief. My back pain continued to be chronic, and my joints continuously ached daily. During the first couple of months of recovery, I tried physical therapy, stem treatments, ultrasound and traction, as well as visiting the chiropractor. I was talking to a friend one day who suggested that I try a massage therapist. The place I was working was in a small, rural setting with not many resources. To my surprise, I was told there was a massage therapist about 15 minutes outside of town. I followed up on this and made an appointment with the massage therapist. I was surprised to find out that not only was she a massage therapist, but she was also certified to teach and train others for certification.

After my first visit, I set up regular visits' multiple times per week. After the first few weeks, I could tell a difference in the healing of my body. As a matter of fact, out of all the treatments and options I tried, massage therapy seemed to help my body heal more than any other method. This was a treatment I would rely on over the years to come.

I spent the remainder of the spring continually receiving treatment and riding the exercise bike. As the weather turned warmer. I was ready to take my ride back out on the roads. Part of me was glad to get back out and ride the new road bike I had purchased. There was also a part of me which was afraid and nervous due to the trauma of the past several months. One thing I always appreciated was my superintendent and friend understanding how emotionally difficult my first ride would be. He made sure to volunteer to be a part of my first ride. This offer was needed and gave me courage and confidence, knowing on my first ride I would not be alone.

Later in the summer my friend (superintendent) and I traveled to Missouri, and we participated in the Tour De Corn. I completed the entire 65 miles and to this day, I am still amazed I was able to complete the ride. Looking back in the years after, I have no doubt my friend and boss set the goal with me so soon after my accident to give me focus, purpose and expectations. It was just as important for him to volunteer to be a part of my first ride back on the roads. This was another life lesson in how to help someone after being through a traumatic event: Offer to be there with him when he is ready to return to the activity which caused so much trauma. His company eased the fear of getting back on the bike.

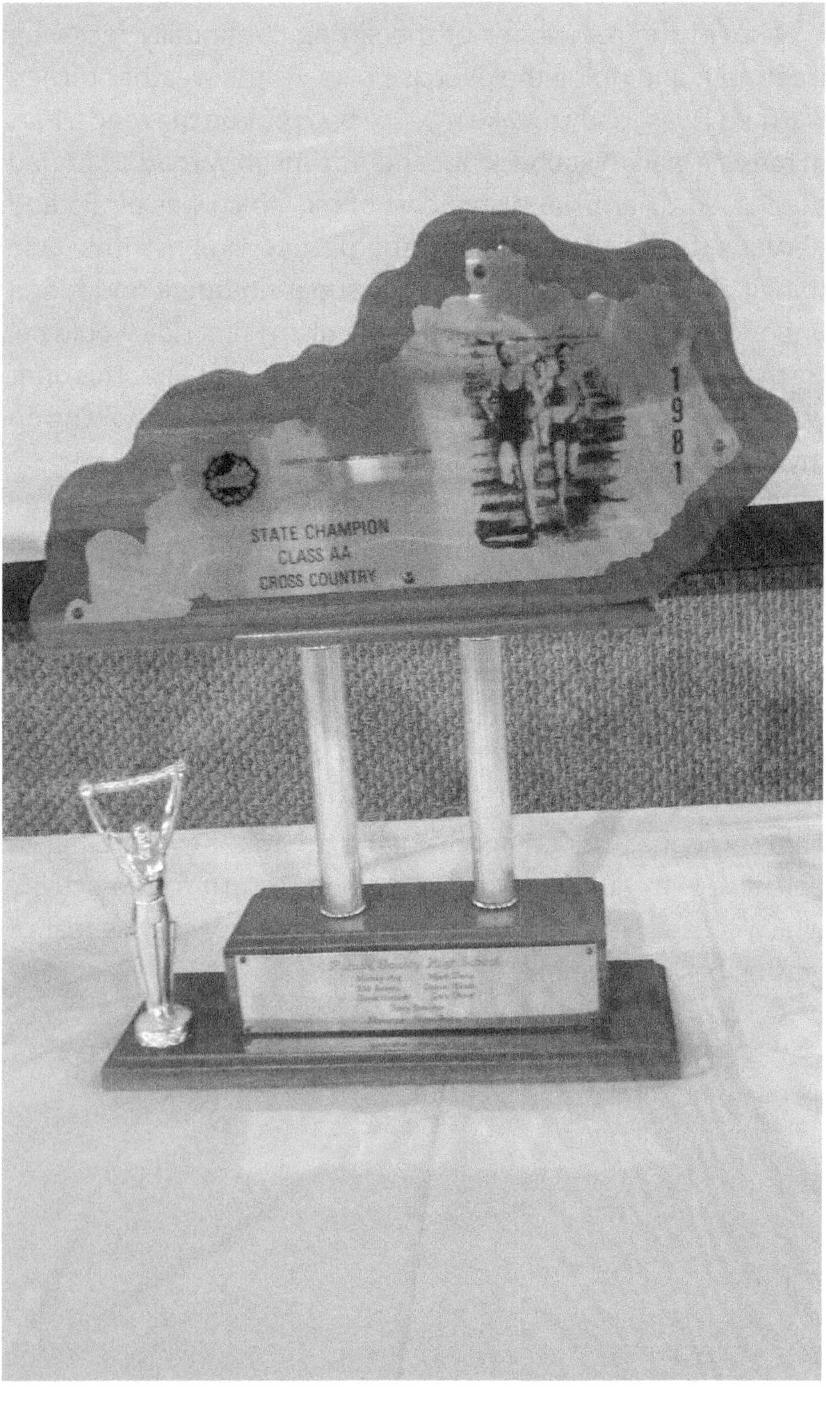

STATE CHAMPION
CLASS AA
CROSS COUNTRY
1981

2
Learn from Your Past

When I was in elementary school, they held tryouts for an annual relay race against the other elementary schools in the city. All fifth-grade students who wanted to try out for the relays would stay after school and run a fifty-yard dash. The fastest 4-8 students would represent our school in a city relay contest. I remember lining up on the sidewalk beside the chain-link fence on our right, which ran along the paved play area behind our school. I was nervous, and it seemed it was taking forever for the line to get smaller and for it to be my turn.

Each student took a turn one at a time and was timed and recorded on how fast they could run a 50-yard dash. It seemed so official at the time for one of our schoolteachers to hold a stopwatch in one hand and raise the other hand. Finally, the arm above the head would drop, and the student would run as fast as he or she could past where the teacher was standing. I always wanted to run fast and be one of the faster students. I thought of myself as a fast runner. I really wanted to make this relay team. My turn finally came, and I ran as fast as I could. Next, it was a matter of waiting to see who the fastest students were to make the relay team. As the results were finally announced, my name was not called. This was one of the first times in my life where I experienced failure. It is a little harsh associating failure with an elementary 50-yard dash. The truth is, I felt like a failure. I wasn't fast enough, and it embarrassed me not to make the team.

What is interesting about this first experience of failure is that it contributed a great deal to which direction my life would take over the next decade. I remember thinking, since I wasn't good enough to make the relay team, I was going to practice and get better and faster. As a fifth-grade student, I didn't understand how to train to increase my speed. My Hall of Fame coaching career was years ahead in the future. I had a simple approach: if I could run a long time without walking, I would get better and get stronger. Running more would make me a faster runner was the logic I employed.

Shortly after the 50-yard dash time trial, I decided to start practicing one day. My plan was to try to run to my cousin's house, which was several blocks away from where I lived. The total distance between our houses was at least a mile. At the time I lived in a medium-sized city which was laid out in city blocks covering a large area. I remember my run to my cousins like it was yesterday. As I began running on the sidewalk alongside the street I lived on, it didn't take long for my lungs to start burning. My goal was to run without walking. I remember as I was approaching an intersection at the end of my street, I was hoping the light would be red so I could catch my breath. Thankfully, there were several intersections, and I would get to stop momentarily and catch my breath at a few of them, waiting for cars to go by or a light to change.

Fifty years later, I can still recall the route I ran and the intersections crossed. It wasn't complicated to get to my cousin's house. I spent many days of my childhood there. I did make it to my cousin's house with very little walking. As I approached the house, I felt a sense of accomplishment. I was proud of what I had accomplished. This feeling of accomplishment was short-lived. As I approached, my aunt, who was on the front porch, exclaimed, "What are you doing?". The tone was not positive; it was followed by, "Does your mother know you are here?" I can't remember exactly what I told her, but it did include, "No, Mom doesn't know I am here." I was so excited about my plan to run and get faster, I forgot some key elements, like asking for permission and not realizing my aunt wouldn't let me walk or run back home.

This was one of the first examples in my life where I can think of where I responded to a traumatic event. Granted, not making a relay team wouldn't be any top ten traumatic life events, but disappointment-wise, it was traumatic for me at the time. I was embarrassed, hurt and decided to respond to the feelings of failure. I made a choice: I was going to make myself a faster and better runner. I always asked myself, why or where did the decision come from to practice and get better as a response to what I perceived as failure? This was one of my first memories of disappointment and being resilient as a response.

I realize all our lives and childhoods are filled with learning and discovering what we are good at and what we enjoy. Life is a constant struggle, dealing with difficult situations and disappointment at all stages. Looking back at "your traumatic events," I believe, can be beneficial by seeing how you responded. Notice the consequences of your response. My accident in 2010 wasn't the first traumatic experience of my life. Not making my 5th-grade relay team wasn't my first major disappointment. Making mistakes and not being successful is a natural part of life. Sometimes individuals respond positively to trauma, and sometimes they respond in a negative manner. By the time I was in fifth grade, I had experienced failure, disappointment and trauma to certain degrees.

When I took a close look at what I considered traumatic events and major disappointments, I could see a pattern. Not all my responses to challenges were positive, but there were many similar responses. As I experienced major traumas, I became interested in trying to find out "why" I responded in the manner I did. What prepared me in my life experiences to respond the way I did? Good or bad. Can I find specific examples of events in my past that contributed to handling trauma in a positive manner? How did my parents or guardians handle traumatic events? It is common knowledge that kids' participation in team and individual sports is beneficial. When you view participation through the lens of resiliency, how is resiliency built? Look at Little League baseball: striking out, missing a ground ball and making a bad throw are all examples of "failure" to a certain degree. The coaching, practice and choice to continue allow individuals to get better and see progress. They begin to experience more positive reinforcing actions than negative. Building resilience can be an outcome of youth sports, just as taking piano lessons can provide similar circumstances and help build resilience. What is applicable for adults? Resiliency is key for overcoming trauma. Looking at your past challenges can be revealing.

After experiencing multiple traumatic events, starting with my 2010 cycling accident, I never intentionally looked at my past to identify and analyze my "traumatic" events. One reason most of us don't look back at traumatic events is to avoid the pain. What I have learned is that once I started identifying "my traumatic events" in life and looking at how I responded, a pattern evolved. I could see how each of the events contributed to who I am now, where I am now and how I respond to challenges. By looking back, you can also learn how you want to respond to future situations.

One activity I suggest you do is a simple analysis of traumatic events you have experienced in life. Get out a sheet of paper and, starting with your earliest memories, make a list of the major traumatic events and/or disappointments you experienced. You define what was "traumatic" for you. It is a list of the events which stand out and cause a great deal of pain (emotional and/or physical). For instance, maybe it was a broken bone, a surgery, not making a team, failing a class, being embarrassed in public, being a victim, loss of a family member, loss of a job, injury, divorce... Obviously, trauma takes on a different meaning as you progress through life. The worst trauma a person experiences in life may take place during childhood. The purpose is to generate the list and then take time to think about each event and how you responded: positive or negative. More importantly, under each event, list any valuable learning you gained. What were good decisions? What decisions would you have changed? How did those decisions affect who and where you are today? As you progress through this activity from your early life until your present, I believe you will start to get a picture of how the trauma and your choices contribute to who you are now. More importantly, understanding your past in the present can help you better plan how you want to deal with trauma in the future. This activity provides various benefits for you. It helps you understand that you do have control over how you react to trauma in the future. It can also demonstrate how you persevered and became the person you are today.

Good can come out of traumatic events. My junior year running cross country, our team won the state championship. I had set my goal to become one of the best runners in the state my senior year and earn a scholarship to a state university. My senior season started with the goal in sight but abruptly ended when I was diagnosed with mono during the fall cross country season. I ended up going to a small private college, and during my freshman year, I developed chronic hip issues. I went to doctor after doctor and multiple physical therapists. I even went to the 1984 U.S. Olympic medical facility in Cincinnati, Ohio, to find a solution. So, my college running career never developed; it was one disappointment after another. My response to not being able to run was to go to practice every day and assist where I could. Three years later, I was a paid assistant track and cross-country coach. I followed this up by earning a graduate assistant position at a state university to assist in coaching distance runners while earning my master's. My coaching success as a GA opened a door to get my first teaching job, which included coaching boys and girls track & field and cross country. I met my wife in college while assisting with track & field, and I coached twelve years of high school track & field and cross country. I was inducted into the Kentucky Track & Cross-Country Coaches Association. I was one of seven finalists for the National High School Coaches Association Girls Cross Country National Coach of the Year. My achievements, both professionally and personally, came to fruition after traumatic events.

It became clear that part of my ability to be resilient and overcome major traumas later in life was due to my previous traumatic events and life experiences. I learned there is still hope when your dreams are shattered. Sometimes what you thought were your dreams get replaced by a better version of life for you to live. Making the most out of every situation, whether good or bad, can ultimately end up being rewarding. The path you choose and want may be abruptly interrupted or completely changed. Understanding the constant positive mindset and making the best of the current situation can be even more rewarding and open doors you had no idea were even possible.

3
Post Trauma Impacts & Coping Methods

Soon after my 2010 hit-and-run accident, as I was nestled into the familiar embrace of the couch at my parents' house, my phone vibrated, revealing an unknown number with a Mississippi area code. Intrigued and slightly apprehensive, I decided to answer, only to hear the voice of a Federal Park Ranger, the very one who had responded to my hit-and-run accident. In an instant, my heart pounded fiercely, and a tidal wave of anxiety pulled me back to that harrowing scene.

The Ranger explained that since the incident occurred within a Federal Park, it was deemed a federal crime, and thus his responsibility to investigate. He asked if any new memories of the accident had emerged since my discharge from the hospital. Regrettably, I had no new information to provide. We concluded the call with his assurance that he would keep me informed about the progress of the investigation.

As I ended the call, a swirl of emotions overwhelmed me. Anger surged through my veins, directed squarely at the individual who had left me in such a state of pain and turmoil. "How could he just abandon me like that?" I thought, wrestling with questions that seemed to have no immediate resolution. This anger gradually morphed into a profound sense of grief, leaving me feeling utterly fragmented, both physically and mentally. I couldn't shake the haunting thought of whether we would ever uncover the identity of the person responsible for this calamity.

Trauma exerts a profound impact on an individual, affecting both his emotional and physical well-being. It can manifest in a myriad of ways, such as through vivid flashbacks and challenges within personal relationships. I distinctly remember an incident that unfolded several months after my accident when I spent most weekends in Somerset. During this period, I would rise early on Monday mornings and embark on the two-hour drive to school.

One morning, while enroute to work, I had just merged onto the interstate highway about thirty minutes into my journey. Out of nowhere, a sudden and intense flashback of my accident overwhelmed me. In my mind, I was back on my bike on the Natchez Parkway, approaching the spot where I intended to make a U-turn to head back to my parents. As I glanced over my left shoulder to check for oncoming traffic, the front end of a truck appeared out of nowhere. Suddenly, there was a collision, and everything went black. It felt as if I had been transported back to that fateful moment, reliving the event in its entirety.

The flashback was so distressing that I was compelled to pull over to the shoulder of the interstate. After putting my vehicle in park, tears began streaming down my face. I sat there, crying, vividly recalling the sensation of being on that road and later waking up lying on the grass. It was as if these flashbacks were piecing together my fragmented memories of the accident. It was the first time I had ever seen the actual truck hitting me. I remained beside the interstate until the emotional wave subsided, allowing me to collect myself and continue my drive to school.

These flashbacks would occur sporadically, each one providing a glimpse of another aspect of my accident. This experience was both confusing and stressful, as I often wondered whether I was seeing actual fragments of my accident or if my mind was fabricating these visions. The flashbacks persisted for two to three years or more after 2010, serving as a constant reminder of the trauma I had endured.

Another aspect of trauma is intrinsically tied to the decision-making process of that day. Even now, I find myself constantly replaying the choices I made regarding my ride and the route I selected. Why did I choose to ride that specific route in December 2010? On that day, I began my journey from my parents' house and rode about three miles to an on-ramp leading to the Natchez Trace Parkway. Upon reaching the parkway, I decided to head north and traveled approximately nine miles before turning around to return home. As I neared the exit ramp to leave the parkway, I glanced at my odometer and realized that if I just rode one more mile south and then turned around, I could complete a 20-mile ride for the day. Tragically, it was during this additional mile I was struck from behind on the parkway, very close to the turnaround point. To this day, I question myself, asking, "Why couldn't I settle for 18 miles?" One extra mile set off a chain of events that drastically altered the course of my life in countless ways. The decision to pursue that additional mile down the parkway has haunted me since. I also could have chosen to get on the Natchez Trace closer to where my parents lived. Why didn't I pick the closer option? No matter how illogical it is to question your decision-making, it is a natural response. Knowing about one different choice could have prevented an inconceivable amount of pain. This is similar thinking to the baseball pitcher who gives up a walk-off home run to lose a game. The "Why did I have to throw that specific pitch?" This is the same type of thinking except the stakes are much higher after a traumatic accident such as a hit-and-run. Nonetheless, both situations cause a great deal of mental grief.

One of the transformative moments in my life occurred during my rehabilitation following my 2010 accident. My body endured significant physical trauma, resulting in constant daily pain, particularly from the compression fractures in my spine. The prospect of needing future spinal surgery loomed over me due to the extensive damage. Therefore, during my rehabilitation, I dedicated myself to strengthening my body to delaying this possibility of surgery for as long as possible.

In the years following the accident, I took immense pride in my recovery journey. I managed to get back on my bicycle just months afterward, a testament to my determination and resilience. Over the next four years, I continued to ride consistently, and by 2014, I achieved some of the best cycling performances of my life. I was riding more miles and at a faster pace than in any previous years, marking a significant milestone in my recovery and personal growth

Unfortunately, my riding experience would eventually become plagued with pain and a significant amount of discomfort. I began to suffer from nerve pain due to the damage in my back, which progressively worsened with each passing day. This nerve damage led to muscle atrophy in my arms and chest, causing the pain to become unbearable.

I vividly recall the first episode of nerve pain I encountered. By 2014, I had transitioned to a new job, working at the college from which I graduated, in a federal grant program. I was living in a college-owned property on the outskirts of the campus.

One night, I awoke to an excruciating pain that started in my neck and traveled down my back, behind my shoulder blade and into the back of my arm. This was a completely new and intense type of pain that I had never experienced before. It was so severe that my instinct was to escape it. I literally started to get up and go somewhere to escape the pain.

It was past 3:00 a.m., and I couldn't bear sitting there in agony any longer. So, I headed out the door, thinking that at least by walking, I could keep myself moving and distract my mind with other thoughts. All I wanted was for the pain to stop.

The following morning, I decided to book an appointment with a massage therapist, hoping that a massage might offer some much-needed relief. I visited a reputable, certified massage business that same morning. As I lay face down on the table, the pain continued to radiate from my neck, under my shoulder blade and down my arm.

The therapist began to work on the affected area, but instead of alleviating the pain, it seemed to intensify, especially as the therapist focused on my neck and shoulder. Within what felt like 20-30 seconds I had to abruptly ask the therapist to "please stop." I sat up, realizing that the massage was not going offer the relief I had hoped. Despite expressing my gratitude to the therapist, I left the appointment feeling more discomfort than before. Panic began to set in as the pain became increasingly unbearable. It was clear that I needed to contact my doctor and physical therapist to inform them of this new and distressing development.

After enduring a traumatic event, I discovered that the long-term physical repercussions on my body necessitated a mindset committed to continuous learning and exploration in pursuit of pain management and body maintenance. I diligently researched specific stretches tailored to the areas of my body that were causing discomfort. One week, I might face hip flexor issues, while the next week might bring challenges with my hamstrings, followed by troubles with my arms. Despite these challenges, I endeavored to maintain a balanced approach in managing all the various pains. The reality was that as long as I continued cycling and enhancing my fitness in this area, I felt content. In fact, achieving new milestones in cycling provided such positive reinforcement that it effectively shifted my focus away from the daily discomfort.

In my journey of navigating mental and emotional challenges, I continually developed coping mechanisms to maintain resilience. One significant strategy I adopted was the decision to forgo taking pain medication. I believed that by proving to myself that I could endure without this aid, I was showcasing a strong mental and physical fortitude. I understood that my body's condition would eventually necessitate major surgery and likely require pain management in the future. However, for the time being, this approach served as a small victory, a way to affirm to myself that I was prevailing against the odds.

Emotionally, I had to devise strategies to cope with the dramatic changes in my life following the hit-and-run incident. The initial months were fraught with anger and anxiety, as I grappled with the uncertainty of not knowing who was responsible for hitting me and why they left the scene. A couple of months after the accident, I received an unexpected call from the ranger who was investigating the case. He informed me that the person responsible had been identified and would be charged in a federal court. I was astonished, having mentally prepared myself for the likelihood that I might never find out the identity of the perpetrator. The ranger explained the meticulous process through which he had identified the suspect. On the day I was hit, he had collected a large piece of broken glass, likely from the truck's lights that hit me. With persistence, he visited every auto repair shop in the vicinity of Tupelo, showing them the piece of glass and requesting notification if anyone came in to replace a light. Remarkably, one of the body shops later contacted him about a truck that had been brought in for repairs with matching broken glass. When the ranger compared the glass from the accident site with the damaged light, it fit perfectly, confirming the truck's involvement.

This revelation was a significant relief, providing me with a sense of closure and easing my emotional turmoil. However, my joy was short-lived when I learned that the individual responsible only received a fine and a suspended license. To add to my frustration, the driver was uninsured, which meant there would be no financial restitution for the crime. Despite these disappointments, the discovery brought a positive outcome by eliminating the agonizing uncertainty of not knowing who had hit me. The motive behind their actions, however, remains a mystery we will never know.

In the aftermath of the accident, grappling with both physical and emotional repercussions proved to be challenging. I was determined to find ways to demonstrate my resilience and ability to triumph over this life-altering event. One coping mechanism I embraced was the establishment of an annual ceremonial ride. Each year, at precisely 2:30 PM on December 22, the exact date and time of my accident, I embarked on this meaningful ride. This ritual became a symbol of my strength and determination, showcasing that I refused to let the accident hinder my passion for riding.

The ceremonial ride evolved into a significant tradition within my yearly routine, serving as a testament to my ability to overcome adversity. Emotionally, it held immense significance, as it commemorated my journey of healing and reaffirmed my commitment to moving beyond the profound impact of the accident. Physically, demonstrating I could still reach new high levels of cycling fitness was a psychological boost. I was a better cyclist than any previous time of my life despite my upper body losing muscle and strength from nerve damage. I did a great job delaying the surgery, but the signs were present it couldn't be ignored much longer.

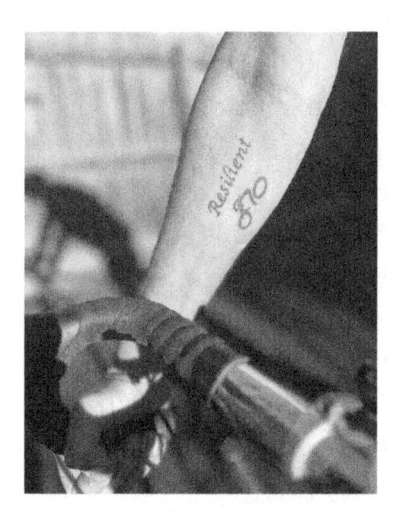

4
Eight Years Was Long Enough

As I was being rolled down the hallway in my bed after my surgery, I was emotionally distraught, crying and repeating over and over, "Why did he have to hit me?" It was as though all of the pain and suffering that had taken place the previous eight years was all coming out at the same time. As I was rolled into my room, my wife and father were there waiting for me. My wife was immediately trying to console me, but it was to no avail. I just kept bawling and crying out, "Why did he have to hit me?" The nurse informed my family members in the room that I was having a bad reaction to the anesthesia used during the surgery.

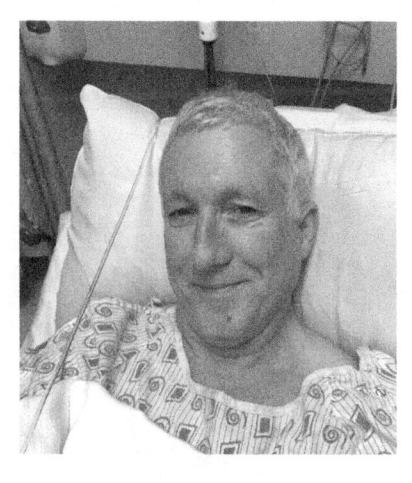

For eight long years, I had carried the heavy burden of my past, a trauma that had become an unwelcome companion in life. I often found myself trapped in a cycle of fear and uncertainty, each day eventually became a battle to simply survive the pain. As the years passed my spinal damage and ability to postpone a major surgery was over. I realized that eight years was long enough. So, the surgery was scheduled, performed and successful on November 15, 2018.

I knew well in advance that this traumatic event would be taking place. This gave me time to understand the procedure and the risks. More importantly, I understood the significant rehab that would need to take place after such extensive surgery. The procedure I would be having was a multilevel cervical discectomy and fusion. In layman's terms, that meant they were going to remove multiple discs in my neck and replace them with small artificial cages in a type of natural cement. Over several months, the substance would harden and protect my spinal cord.

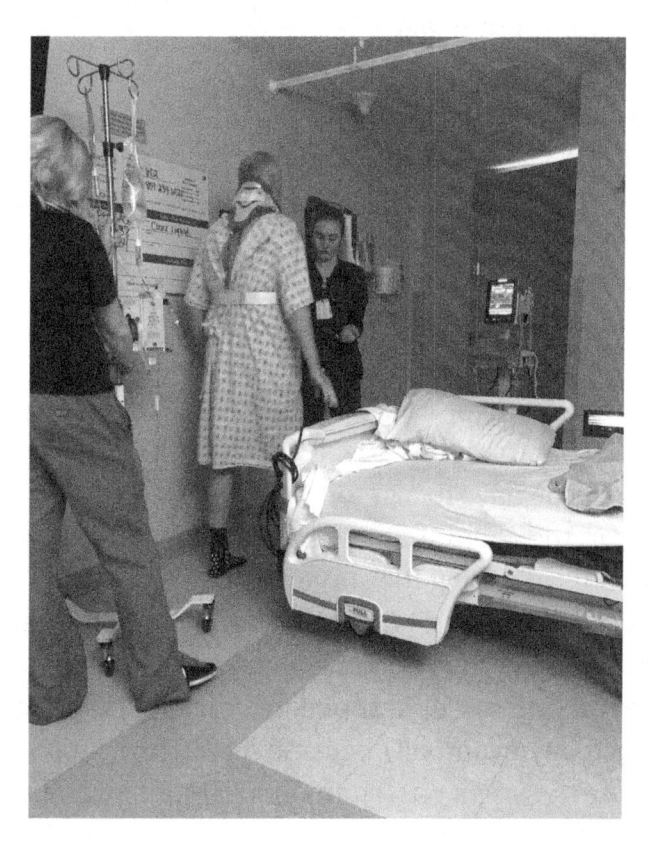

Once I transitioned into the room and calmed down, I can remember how difficult it was to swallow and talk. I was feeling this way because my esophagus had to be moved to access the vertebrae for the surgery. For every minute that I woke up, I started realizing how horrible I felt. This was another similar moment in my life where the clock was my only ally. In the early days, the only way I could find relief was by sleeping and being medicated.

I eagerly anticipated the solace of sleep, as it offered an escape from the relentless pain and a chance for my body to heal. Despite all the preparation and research I had done to understand what to expect from the surgery, nothing could truly prepare me for the actual pain and discomfort that ensued. Having spent considerable time in hospital settings before, I was no stranger to enduring significant pain. My focus became a matter of surviving hour by hour.

Even after my transition home a few days later, the situation remained unchanged in terms of pain. I was confronted with a level of discomfort and a threshold of pain that I had only experienced once before, following my accident in 2010. Had you asked me two weeks' post-surgery whether it was worth it, I would have unequivocally said no. The thought of enduring such agony again, even for the promise of eliminating my nerve pain, was unfathomable at that moment.

The initial days at home were primarily focused on managing pain and reducing the swelling from the surgery. Fortunately, I had been discharged from the hospital with a special cooler. This cooler was equipped with a tube that connected to a cold pack, allowing ice water to continually circulate through it. This ingenious setup provided consistent and long-lasting cold therapy to the affected area, significantly aiding in my recovery.

Reflecting on my experience from eight years ago, when I was rehabilitating from an accident, I remembered the crucial importance of staying active as soon as possible. Each day, I made it a priority to move around and walk as much as I could to stimulate blood circulation, which is essential for the healing process. Maintaining mobility was also vital in preventing the formation of blood clots. As a precaution, I was administering a daily injection in my abdomen to avert blood clots, a routine that needed to be sustained for a month or more.

Another similarity I had been accustomed to years earlier was the necessity to depend on others for most of my basic needs. Although I was able to get up and move around, there were still very few tasks I could accomplish independently. One of the most significant challenges was eating regular food due to the difficulty of swallowing. Certain foods, like breads, would often get lodged in my throat and wouldn't go down as effortlessly as others. Consequently, each meal became an experiment, a trial-and-error process to determine which foods could be swallowed with ease. I was informed that this was a normal occurrence and could persist for months.

Following my surgery in 2018, I remained resolutely determined to approach my rehabilitation with intense dedication. I set a clear goal for myself: to get back on a bicycle as soon as possible. To better prepare myself for this milestone, I committed to walking every day. I utilized the same app, Strava, which I typically use to track my cycling rides, to record my daily walks. This allowed me to monitor my progress, and witnessing tangible improvements gave me a significant boost in confidence.

The expected time frame for when I would be cleared to resume biking was approximately three months. This period was necessary to ensure that my fragile neck had sufficient time for the fusion to solidify. Fortunately, my surgeon, who had a unique perspective due to his brother being a professional cyclist, understood the mental significance of returning to cycling for enthusiasts like me. Recognizing the progress I made in my rehabilitation, he granted me permission to get back on a bike on January 7, 2019. This was a momentous occasion for me, as it marked my return to cycling just shy of two months post-surgery.

During my first ride, I remember rolling out of my driveway and heading down the street toward the four-lane road. Mentally, it felt incredible to be back on the bike; it was a significant milestone. However, physically, sitting upright felt strange. I couldn't lower myself to the drop handlebars due to the stiffness in my neck. So, I decided to choose a route that required very little looking over my shoulder, allowing me to focus on pedaling and savor the ride.

After four or five miles, I managed to find a decent rhythm and discovered a position for my neck that minimized irritation. In the back of my mind, I was aware of the potential danger a fall could pose, given the fragility of my neck, yet I chose not to dwell on this concern and instead concentrated on the joy of being back on the bike.

Fortunately, on January 7th, the weather was favorable enough for my outdoor ride. As I turned off the four-lane road back into my subdivision, I experienced a whirlwind of emotions: relief and satisfaction from completing the ride, but also the sobering reality of the long road ahead to regain my previous level of cycling fitness. I had doubts about whether I had any good years of cycling remaining. Maybe my best years were in my past? I was also worried about how much my neck would improve in the coming months. Was I going to have better neck movement than now? What if it was always like this? These concerns ran through my mind.

One of the profound challenges following my 2010 accident was grappling with depression. The persistent pain inflicted by someone else's actions was a constant mental burden, especially on days when the pain became unbearable. My struggle with depression intensified unexpectedly after my 2018 surgery. There were days filled with triumph, as I achieved milestones like cycling 15 miles, and on those days, I felt invincible. Yet, there were also days when I plummeted into despair, waking up to excruciating pain and contemplating the drastic changes my life had undergone over the past eight years. Reflecting on the myriads of challenges I had faced often left me feeling trapped and despondent. During these low periods, I found it incredibly difficult to motivate myself to engage in any activity. I felt paralyzed, unable to commit to rehabilitation, cycling, attending doctor's appointments, or participating in physical therapy.

What compounded the difficulty of battling depression during these times was my reluctance to share my feelings with others. I tended to withdraw, avoiding conversations about my internal struggles. This isolation made it hard for me to envision a future, given everything I had endured. At my lowest, I was caught in a relentless cycle that began with anger, transitioned through feelings of injustice, and culminated in a sense of hopelessness.

One of the most challenging aspects of surviving a traumatic event is the lingering grip it maintains long after the event has passed. It never quite relinquishes its hold, continually casting a shadow over one's life.

I have been on a journey to tackle depression and navigate through challenging days by employing various strategies that I've learned over time. Setting goals has been an anchor for me, providing a positive focus and helping to keep the depression at bay. Cycling has also been a significant source of motivation, driving me to regain my fitness level prior to my surgery. I find any regular physical activity is a positive reinforcement for me. If I am moving, putting forth effort and making progress, I can keep depression at bay.

Occasionally, hearing about a tragedy in the news can shake me emotionally, serving as a stark reminder that things could always be worse. These moments encourage me to transform my depression into a catalyst for renewed focus and motivation. There is undeniable power in recognizing the struggles of others; it serves as a poignant reminder of how fortunate I am.

At times, I have felt guilty for allowing myself to be depressed and down about my life, especially when I consider the reality that I never fully understood how I managed to survive the challenges I've faced. Survival guilt is a real emotion which can feed the cycle of depression if you don't acknowledge its impact. I've learned to channel these feelings into a force for positive change, reminding myself many would like to be where I am today. Some were not fortunate to survive traumatic events such as mine. This approach celebrates my resilience and capacity for growth.

Another area of concern was the impact on my wife, son and daughter. My daughter dealt with the stress by focusing on my needs once I got home. She handled things better by being there physically and making sure she could support my wife caring for me. My son had a career and family to focus on, which I was glad about, because my trauma hit him hard emotionally. I really believe my accident in 2010 caused him more emotional grief because he had arrived at my accident site and witnessed his father being put in an ambulance seriously injured. My surgery and pain I believe was a reminder of what he witnessed. My wife continued to amaze me. Her focus was totally on taking care of my needs. She never wavered from focusing on my care. I knew it was exhausting for her but she was wired differently than others. It didn't matter how tired she was physically or mentally, my needs were put first. I never understood how she could go through this without a meltdown in front of me. I worried about how my trauma interrupted my family's lives.

Two months after my surgery, I experienced a significant turning point in my recovery. I began to feel much more like myself, regaining a sense of continuity in my daily activities. Whether it was riding outdoors or exercising on a stationary bike, I was making strides in improving my fitness. There were so many hours in the day when I wasn't active. Even when things were going well, having too much downtime, both mentally and physically, wasn't necessarily beneficial.

Since I couldn't return to work yet, I found myself struggling to make use of my free time productively. I decided to explore new interests and stumbled upon the fascinating world of drones. The potential they held for generating additional income intrigued me. I had never considered myself particularly tech-savvy, nor had I imagined venturing into something as unfamiliar as starting a drone business. Yet, I found myself drawn to the challenge.

During this period of downtime, I dedicated my efforts to researching various types of drones, learning about the process of becoming a licensed drone operator and understanding the steps involved in launching a business in this field. This endeavor proved to be an excellent way to keep myself mentally engaged and served as a powerful deterrent to depression. It provided me with a sense of purpose and something new to strive toward. I was motivated by the opportunity to acquire new knowledge and skills. Just learning about specific drones provided days and weeks of research. I wasn't in a hurry or even making a conscious decision about starting a drone business. I needed to learn about drones, buy one and learn how to fly one. This process I found interesting, and it helped me use whatever free time I had to be active mentally.

I believe, subconsciously, that I was always searching for something to occupy my mind and attention when I was unable to ride or physically exert myself. Movement was such an important part of my life, the long stretches of inactivity I experienced after 2010, and my surgery 2018 were difficult time periods, not only due to the pain, but the inability to move which provided me with an outlet. I am thankful after 2010 my outlook toward trying new things totally changed. I was more open than ever to learning new skills and putting aside fear or hesitancy. I bought new tools and became much handier doing my own maintenance and projects. Prior to 2010 I did not have the confidence or patience to try challenging skills outside of my comfort zone.

This new freedom of not being afraid to try new things opened a whole new world for me. I became much more reliant on my own abilities and willingness to learn. My interest in drones began post-surgery in 2019. The interest and passion continued to grow and a few years later I launched my very own RoBo Drone Services LLC. Utilizing down time after trauma to acquire new knowledge and skills is a great strategy which also can keep depression in check. Filling your free time with something positive is another strategy which pays big dividends.

5
The Illusion of Closure

On the crisp morning of September 10, 2020, I found myself at the visitor center just outside Asheville, NC right next to the breathtaking Blue Ridge Parkway. Life felt truly magnificent. Having fully recovered from my surgery in 2018, I was looking forward to an exceptional year of cycling adventures. My wife and I decided to rent a cabin nestled near Asheville, providing the perfect setting for a peaceful and rejuvenating vacation. One of the ambitious goals on my bucket list was to go on a cycling journey from Asheville to Mount Mitchell and back. This formidable 40-mile round trip posed a challenge, with the initial 20 miles being a relentless uphill climb.

Eager to conquer this challenge, I set off from the visitor center and soon began the ascent, quickly finding a steady and satisfying rhythm. The morning was idyllic, with minimal traffic and a refreshingly cool temperature that made the climb not only manageable but enjoyable. After approximately 10 miles, I reached a picturesque scenic overlook, offering a perfect opportunity to pause and marvel at the vistas of the Blue Ridge Mountain range. With each pedal stroke, as I climbed higher and closer to Mount Mitchell, the view unfolded into increasingly stunning panoramas, each more breathtaking than the last.

Instead of succumbing to fatigue from the relentless ascent, I was invigorated, boosted by the fitness I had acquired despite the challenges of recent years. With each pedal stroke, my anticipation grew, and after a few hours of leaving the visitor center, I reached the summit of Mount Mitchell.

Dismounting, I stood in awe of the breathtaking views of the Blue Ridge Mountains, a beautiful example of nature's splendor stretching before me. I had a profound sense of accomplishment after reaching the summit.

This ride is exactly why I loved cycling. I envisioned my future years riding in a variety of picturesque settings around the country. This ride was better than I ever imagined it being.

I had a shot of adrenalin anticipating the ride down the mountains, I climbed back onto my bicycle, ready to embrace the thrilling descent to the visitor center and onward to Asheville. The 20-mile downhill ride was sheer joy and exhilarating that offered some of the most thrilling moments I've ever experienced on two wheels. On the steeper sections, I reached exhilarating speeds close to 40 miles per hour, while cruising comfortably between 25 and 30 miles per hour.

As I returned to the visitor center, I dismounted and stood still for a moment, sipping water and reflecting on the remarkable journey. I felt a genuine and deep appreciation for every challenge overcome and every moment, culminating in a profound sense of personal achievement. It was an unforgettable day; one marked by nearly two hours of relentless climbing followed by an hour of exhilarating descent.

Reflecting on the past decade, I find myself filled with gratitude for the journey of recovery and resilience I've experienced. At the pinnacle of my cycling fitness, I have successfully left the traumas of 2010 and 2018 behind. This cycling season, I embarked on thrilling adventures, discovering new bike trails in Pittsburgh, PA and enjoying a breathtaking ride along Skyline Drive in the mountains of Virginia. I've returned to my robust routine, effortlessly tackling 40 and 50-mile rides with a strength reminiscent of my peak years.

As I officially close the chapter on a challenging decade marked by trauma, relentless rehabilitation, surgery and yet more rehabilitation, I feel a profound sense of accomplishment. While my body and mind bear the memories of what they've endured, there's an immense joy in having overcome such formidable obstacles. I have once again scaled a mountain of barriers, reached the summit and returned to the activities I cherish most.

Closure is a term often used in the realm of trauma and healing, suggesting a finality or a neat resolution to our emotional wounds. However, the concept of closure can be misleading, as it implies that there is a definitive endpoint to the pain and challenges brought on by traumatic experiences. In truth, the journey of overcoming trauma is less about reaching a destination of complete healing and more about embracing an ongoing process of growth and transformation.

Many individuals find themselves chasing the illusion of closure, believing that if they can just achieve it, the weight of their past will be lifted. This pursuit can be exhausting and disheartening, as it sets an unrealistic expectation for what healing should look like. Instead of seeking closure, it may be more beneficial to focus on integration—finding ways to incorporate the experiences into a broader narrative of personal resilience and strength. This is accomplished more by how we process our thoughts and what we focus our minds on.

Trauma, by its nature, can leave lasting imprints on our psyches, influencing how we perceive the world and interact with others. Rather than striving for an elusive sense of closure, we can shift our perspective to appreciate the resilience that emerges from navigating these scars. By recognizing that healing is not a linear path, we allow ourselves the grace to move forward at our own pace, acknowledging the setbacks and celebrating the triumphs along the way. Recovering from trauma is somewhat a mystery as to how the recovery will be defined and what limits your recovery will reach.

Ultimately, the goal is not to close the chapter on trauma but to learn how to thrive despite it. By relinquishing the notion of closure, we open ourselves to the possibility of a richer, more authentic existence—one that honors our past while embracing the potential of our future. Understanding the process of recovery can be rewarding by enjoying the progress along the way. Putting parameters on an expected level of recovery is setting yourself up for failure. This approach puts you in an "all- or nothing" situation between success and failure.

During my time coaching cross country it was important to teach distance runners not to put "all or nothing" expectations on your performance. Instead, I always told them, "Great preparation, great effort and a great attitude is what you can focus on. This is putting value on the process instead of the result. There is a place for setting goals but not at the expense of failing if the goal isn't accomplished."

On October 20th, 2020, I embarked on a thrilling new adventure as I mounted my mountain bike and left the parking lot behind. As I hit the dirt trail and entered the dense woods, the path began to narrow and descend into a gradual slope peppered with rocks. I stood up on the pedals, allowing my tires to skillfully navigate over the protruding tree roots. The sensation was reminiscent of the familiar jolt of hitting rumble strips on the highway in a vehicle. The trail soon demanded my full attention as it veered sharply to the right, quickly followed by a sudden left turn, leading me into a series of short steep hills that mimicked the ups and downs of a rollercoaster ride. My mind raced, processing what felt like a hundred thoughts per second, as I anticipated the next twist and slope of the trail. As I approached a blind corner, I discovered a narrow wooden bridge awaiting me. With quick reflexes, I aligned myself to cross it, immediately preparing for the steep uphill climb that lay on the other side.

Crossing the bridge, I settled back into the saddle and shifted gears to tackle the challenging ascent. This was my initiation into the exhilarating world of mountain biking, a stark contrast to the road cycling I was accustomed to. This new style of riding engaged an entirely different set of muscles, ones I had yet to fully develop, as I was new to this thrilling discipline. That day marked my very first mountain bike ride, a journey that introduced me to a different kind of bike and a course unlike any I had previously experienced.

A close friend of mine, an experienced and passionate mountain biker, inspired me to explore a new facet of biking. He guided me through the process of acquiring a quality pre-owned mountain bike and the necessary gear to enhance my experience. As I embarked on this journey, my confidence soared, especially after a productive spring and summer of riding. I was thrilled to achieve a level of fitness I hadn't experienced in 3 to 5 years.

Determined to embrace the learning curve of a new sport, I was eager to invest time and effort into discovering the joy that this type of biking brings. Adding to the excitement was the knowledge that a nearby park featured an exceptional series of trails specifically designed for mountain biking. Just a twenty-minute drive away, I could find myself immersed in miles of dirt trails brimming with challenges and in a serene setting. This new adventure not only enriched my physical well-being but also provided me with a sense of mental clarity and satisfaction. I was truly in a great place, both physically and mentally.

The added bonus for mountain biking was that it would enhance my strength, thereby boosting my road cycling performance. Even as a middle-aged adult, I found it exhilarating to seek out ways to gain an edge and improve my skills. It reminded me of my high school days as a distance runner when our coach introduced us to cross-training by incorporating weightlifting sessions three times a week. Back in the late seventies and early eighties, cross-training was not common practice in distance running. However, after a season of combining lifting and running, the benefits and competitive edge became quite apparent. I envisioned mountain biking not just as an enjoyable alternative, but also as a significant asset to enhance my road cycling abilities.

As I have previously mentioned, my past traumatic experiences have profoundly reshaped my perspective on embracing new adventures and seizing the moments and opportunities that life presents. Responding to the traumatic events as opportunities to grow and try new things was a much healthier approach than chasing closure. This transformation instilled in me a renewed appreciation for indulging in activities that I am passionate about. For instance, during a mandatory work trip to a conference in Pittsburgh, PA, I took my road bike with me to explore what the bike trails in Pittsburgh had to offer. Through diligent research, I discovered that Pittsburgh boasts some exceptional riding paths for road bikes. Remarkably, one of these trails can even take you all the way to Washington D.C.

For the very first time, I thought about the opportunities of bringing along my road bike and adding value to the travel experience. I ventured out to explore the city's trails on my bike before and after the daily meetings. Having my bike gave me the opportunity to explore Pittsburgh and see so much more of the city. Since I chose to drive to the conference to take my bike it allowed me to detour after the conference to Skyline Drive. I left the conference in the morning after it concluded and decided to take a detour and take a ride on Skyline Drive. There, I had an unforgettable experience of riding through the mountains of the Shenandoah National Park in Virginia. This trip was a continuation of an extraordinary year filled with remarkable biking adventures. I had a newfound appreciation of cycling and enjoying what it offered.

I was already starting to plan new adventures for road cycling and mountain biking. My family is so dispersed while visiting my parents I would be able to try out some of the mountain biking facilities in Mississippi. My son is living in North Carolina outside of Charlotte, which is renowned for all the mountain biking opportunities in this area and throughout the state. I am ready to enjoy the future of riding.

Traumatic events can cause a person to fall into the trap of chasing closure. It is a natural response to want the physical and emotional pain to end. Trauma is so overwhelming we try to define when it will be over. Changing the mindset and using post traumatic events as opportunities and new experiences is so much better. Don't wish your time away waiting for specific times or events to symbolize closure. I found it refreshing and rewarding to immerse myself in new opportunities and experiences. I found it satisfying knowing I could control my post trauma experiences. The experiences I planned and enjoyed demonstrated how I could thrive in life by focusing on what was possible.

6
The Unthinkable — Is This a Bad Dream?

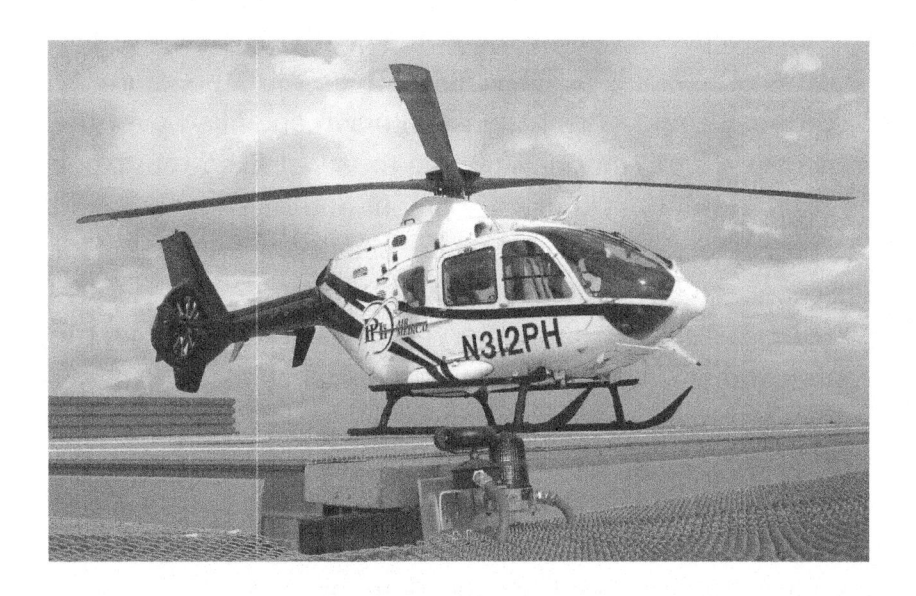

It was Wednesday, November 2, 2020, and I found myself immersed in work. Like many others during the pandemic, I was working from home. Just as my day seemed to blur into a continuous stretch of screen time since 8:00 a.m., I received an email from my boss. Our 2:30 p.m. meeting was canceled, opening an unexpected window of free time. I seized this opportunity to break away from the computer and embark on a bike ride.

Faced with a welcomed dilemma, I thought about the type of ride to undertake. Should I head to the local park and continue my mountain biking adventures on the trails, or opt for the simplicity of a road bike ride? Ultimately, I chose the latter, favoring the efficiency of not having to spend forty minutes going to and coming home from the park. It was an ideal day to cover 20-25 miles, allowing me to return home in time to prepare dinner before my wife arrived from work.

In the garage, I put on my helmet and cycling shoes, ready to hit the road. The only decision left was which route to take. I often decided on my path spontaneously, and that day was no exception. Leaving the subdivision, I reached the main road before making my final choice. There were three familiar directions I could take, each well-known and liked over the past 14 years. On that day, I opted for a well-liked route, one I'd ridden countless times. Feeling fit and relishing the mild weather before winter's chill set in, I pedaled away, grateful for the chance to get out in the sun and enjoy a ride.

A little after 2:00 in the afternoon, I navigated through the center of a small town without the usual concern of heavy traffic. As my route took me downtown, I made the familiar right turn onto East Mount Vernon. In just under a quarter of a mile, I passed through the last traffic light, four blocks beyond the fountain. After clearing the final traffic light, I settled into my usual cruising speed, around 18 mph.

As I scanned the road ahead, I noticed a car a few blocks away slowing down, intending to make a left turn across my path. Approaching the car, I felt assured they had seen me: their left turn signal blinked, and they had come to a complete stop, looking in my direction.

Simultaneously, I observed a vehicle coming to a halt at the street on my right, where the oncoming car was poised to turn.

As I drew nearer, my focus shifted to the SUV emerging from the side street. The SUV stopped and appeared to acknowledge my presence on the main road, especially since the oncoming vehicle was patiently waiting for me to pass before executing its turn. Confident that all potential hazards had been addressed, I proceeded straight ahead.

Bike riders routinely encounter such scenarios, processing a multitude of data points in mere seconds multiple times on every ride. As I neared the intersection, disbelief washed over me as I watched the small SUV begin to pull out onto the street. Instinctively, I stood up on my bike and attempted to brake, but the bike began to wobble from side to side as both brakes locked up the tires, causing the tires to skid. I released the brakes to regain control, but it was too late. I remember attempting to turn sideways while standing to brace for the impending impact. The next moment was filled with a deafening crash...

I vividly remember the moment I crashed into the side of the vehicle, which threw me back toward the pavement. As the back of my head in my helmet struck the ground, I was taken by how soft the landing felt. It was as if I had been laid down gently to protect my head and the hardware in my neck from injury. There was no anticipated slamming of my helmet against the pavement. I was literally amazed at how smooth and soft the sensation of landing was. This sensation remains incredibly clear in my memory, as if it happened just yesterday. That was the very first thought that crossed my mind after the impact as I hit the pavement. I know I lost consciousness for a brief period, but there was no discomfort in doing so. I am sure there are logical interpretations of what I felt. Regardless, it felt like I was in slow motion going to the pavement and gently being placed.

When I came to, I recall someone coming over to help me while I still had the bike between my legs, lying on the street. There was a lot of activity around me, and within a couple of minutes, I heard sirens from the firehouse, which was only a stone's throw away, a few blocks from where I lay on the pavement. I didn't know who the pedestrians were who tried to ask me if I was alright. They wanted to know if I could use their help and get up. Someone started to lift the bike up to remove it from between my legs. I remember yelling in pain, "Stop, my foot is still attached to the pedal." The attempted lifting of the bike sent a huge sharp pain up my side. Upon hearing my shouting, they gently laid the bike back down.

The first responders were firefighters and emergency personnel who quickly arrived at the scene shortly after the bystanders tried to move the bike off me. One of them immediately assessed my condition and potential injuries. They were talking to me, trying to get me alert and answer questions. I don't recall exactly the questions, but I remember telling them my shoe is still attached to the pedal and would have to be dislodged before moving the bike. I tried to turn my ankle out, which would unclip the shoe from the pedal. There was a sharp pain with the movement, making me wince, but it unclipped. Any attempt to move my body and get me to be lying on my back was causing horrible pain. The ambulance had just pulled up after the painful attempt to move me. The first responders yelled at the ambulance personnel to bring a backboard with the stretcher.

They carefully slid a backboard underneath me. I was in a great deal of pain in my midsection and right leg as they prepared me for the board. The responders gently slid the board underneath me, and four of the first responders lifted me and placed me on the stretcher and loaded me into the back of the ambulance. As we left the scene, they began starting IVs and hooking up monitors. Everything had happened so fast that I finally noticed the siren blaring as we left the scene to go to the hospital. Throughout the ride to the hospital, I remained conscious and was mentally envisioning what street we were on going toward the hospital. I asked one of the paramedics to call my wife and inform her of the accident so she could be at the hospital as soon as possible. After I gave her number, I realized I was in a familiar position and was reliving a ride in an ambulance ten years earlier during the same month. Did the unthinkable just happen to me again? The whole situation seemed like a bad dream. My worst nightmare was coming true. I was hit on a bicycle for the second time.

The urgency and flurry of activities on the way to the hospital kept me from dwelling on the fact that I was repeating an unthinkable event. Upon my arrival at the hospital, I had little time to process what I was going through. The entire experience was overwhelming and surreal, and there was a seriousness I couldn't help but pick up on from the paramedics concerning my condition.

Once I arrived at the hospital, I knew I would be taken for tests to determine the extent of my injuries. Honestly, I don't remember any of the MRIs or X-rays they performed on me. My next memory was being brought back to a room where my wife was waiting. I truly don't know whether she was waiting or if she got there and I was already in the room but not conscious.

There is never a good time for an accident, but at least this one happened in my hometown. It was comforting to know that my primary care physician was nearby and fully aware of my current and past medical history. I was also comforted knowing my wife's work location was only a mile or two from the hospital. She would have no difficulty getting there quickly. I can't recall the conversation that took place between my wife and me while waiting for a doctor for the results of my tests. I know we were talking, but there was a certain amount of shock and disbelief about what was going on.

In what felt like only a few minutes, the doctor came in and began to talk to us about my injuries. He explained that my pelvis was fractured in multiple places, there was a suspected concussion and my right hip was dislocated. His main concern was that I had internal bleeding around the pelvis. He suggested that I be flown to the University of Kentucky as soon as possible. At this point, I was scared and vividly remember the fear of not knowing the severity of bleeding. I was panicking on the inside but remaining as strong as possible on the outside for my wife.

Right after the doctor gave his recommendations, my primary care physician walked into the room. I immediately asked him if he thought it was necessary to be flew to Lexington. His response was firm "yes." I could see the concern and seriousness in his face and in the tone of his voice. I did get a certain amount of relief when my doctor showed up. I had trust in him and if he said I needed to be flown to the University of Kentucky Hospital, that was all I needed. The next several minutes consisted of waiting for the helicopter and all the arrangements to be made by the hospital prior to the flight. My wife and I had time to talk and plan. We were trying to make sure family members were informed of what was happening. My wife was also trying to plan the drive to the hospital and everything she might need. I informed her my wallet was in my truck at home and asked if she could get someone to go pick it up for our son. It seemed absurd for me to worry about where my wallet was, but really, I told them in case things didn't go well and I didn't get the chance to; it was nervous energy. Soon I found myself on a stretcher being wheeled to the helicopter on the helipad. My wife and I had just said our goodbyes to each other. Fortunately, my son was at the hospital and was a support for my wife to get prepared and start the drive to University of Kentucky Medical Center.

Suddenly, the reality of the situation hit me as I was loaded into the helicopter. My flight was going to take 35-40 minutes, but my wife wouldn't be at the UK hospital for at least an hour and a half, closer to two hours. My mind raced with anxious thoughts like, "What if I never get to see her, my son, or daughter again?" and "What if the bleeding is severe and I don't make it to the hospital?" The fear was overwhelming, yet the physical pain was starting to dominate my attention. Looking back, the pain distracting me from worrying was a good thing. I had a huge lump in my throat, imagining the worst-case scenario.

As soon as I was loaded onto the helicopter, they administered an injection for the pain. Almost immediately, I could feel some relief. The stretcher I was on was positioned behind the right shoulder of the pilot; one flight medic was on my left, and another was situated near my feet. Turning my head to the left, I had a clear view of the sky. I had no sense of how much time had passed since the accident, but I knew it was late enough in the day to see the supermom as I gazed out of the helicopter window. The flight medic beside me directed me to look at this unusual sight.

Being in so much pain, I had no interest in sightseeing. After the flight medic's urging, I took in the view. The brief enjoyment was quickly replaced by pain. I asked the medic if I could receive another injection. The pain was so intense. He informed me that he would administer another dose right before we landed, which would be in about 5-10 minutes. Desperate to escape the pain, I mentally retreated to one of my strategies I'd used ten years earlier in my first cycling accident. I retreated mentally, imagining myself running the GE cross-country course. It was a familiar place I visited to escape the present pain, and I would rely on this until we landed. As we started to land, I turned my thoughts toward my wife and family. I prayed they would arrive safely, and I would still be around to see them. The unknown during this period was emotionally challenging. I got another injection for pain, in anticipation of the need to move me multiple times and the pain that would accompany each movement of my body.

I remember disembarking from the helicopter and being swiftly escorted inside the building by medical personnel. At that point, I was oblivious to my surroundings due to the heavy pain medications I had just been administered. My next memory is of being wheeled into a makeshift room; its walls were comprised of mere sheets, hanging up as temporary walls. The floors were concrete, giving the feeling we were in a basement-type environment. As confusing as this environment was, I immediately forgot about it as I saw my wife standing beside my bed. My fears of not seeing her again were gone.

During the height of the pandemic, the hospital set up these makeshift rooms to manage overcrowding and to separate COVID-19 patients from non-COVID patients. The atmosphere was chaotic. I was in such excruciating pain that I didn't care. I only wanted more pain relief and to find out if the internal bleeding was under control.

My sense of time was distorted under the circumstances, but I do recall eventually being moved to a private room that resembled a conventional hospital room. It was not a typical room on a specific floor with room after room. This room was off to itself but equipped like a typical room. I felt a wave of relief knowing my wife was there and I was stable, awaiting the results of my most recent tests. Mentally, I began to grasp the full extent of what had happened and the reality of my current situation. We eagerly awaited the latest results from the doctors.

Finally, we received encouraging news that my internal bleeding had slowed down and was not life-threatening. I knew this was great news for my wife and me, but I had little time to feel good about it due to the incredible pain. I knew this feeling all too well, feeling so miserable I was on the verge of vomiting or passing out. My ally at this point was the medication to put me to sleep. I learned over the past ten years that sometimes medication and sleep are your only refuge from pain. I had experience of being in this exact situation. It was time to be reacquainted with "Pain."

7
My Old Friend "Pain"

The entire day and night of the accident felt like it lasted for a week. The very next morning, I had already transitioned to being miserable with pain. The shock of the accident was wearing off due to all the attention and anxiety being given to the internal bleeding issue. A doctor came by first thing in the morning to give an update on the internal bleeding and finally to start discussing the treatment for my dislocated hip.

The bleeding remained slow, and the expectation was that it would subside on its own. Next, he moved on to explain the procedure concerning my dislocated hip. First, it would require putting my right leg in traction and applying a great deal of tension to pull my leg back down into place. The procedure was to be done in my room, and I had no idea what was to come. I found myself in the unfortunate position of being reacquainted with pain but in a way that I had never experienced before.

As they began preparing me for the procedure, I was administered pain medication through the IV, along with numbing injections above my knee. They instructed my wife that she would need to leave the room during the procedure. The process started with their using a DeWalt drill to create a hole from the inside of my right leg, about two inches above my knee, all the way through to the other side so a steel rod could be inserted.

I was surprised when I saw the DeWalt drill. I couldn't imagine it was to be used as part of the procedure. To my disbelief, it was the tool being used. Two cables would then be attached to each side of the steel rod and be connected to weights at the foot of the bed on the floor. This would provide continuous pulling, eventually bringing my hip back down into the socket. As the drilling began, I couldn't decide whether I was going to get sick to my stomach or pass out. I had experienced this before on multiple occasions. This time was different. I could distinctly feel the difference when the drill penetrated a tendon compared to muscle. The tendon provided much more resistance for the drill bit, whereas the muscle was quite easy and smooth for the drill bit to go through. I couldn't determine if the physical pain was worse or if the mental agony of understanding what was happening was more unbearable. While the drilling was underway, I had to look and confirm I wasn't dreaming about what was happening. I wasn't dreaming!

Over the past decade, I had become no stranger to pain, but this experience introduced me to a level of pain I had never known. It seems every time I have been subjected to incredible pain, during my 2010 accident or 2018 surgery, I come away thinking pain could never be worse. Yet, here I am, after being hit by a second vehicle, and I am experiencing another whole new level of pain. I resorted to one of the few strategies I knew:

mentally transporting myself to a cross-country race from my past while the procedure took place. I have relied on this mental strategy many times over the years. Whether I was running a race or doing a hard workout, the key was to focus my mind on something as far removed from the current situation as possible. Even though I was mentally focusing on running a cross-country race, I had tears leaking out of each eye, running down my cheeks. I stayed mentally focused on re-running a race from my high school days. The entire procedure probably took around ten to fifteen minutes from start to finish. Once it was over, my relief was short-lived.

Within a few minutes after the procedure had been completed, and my wife had returned to the room, I realized the pain was going to be constant due to the pressure exerted by the cables on the steel pin for pulling my hip down. I wish I could tell you that I was mentally prepared and had a strategy to escape the pain, but I discovered from past experiences that while you can endure pain for a short period by mentally retreating somewhere, you can't do that for every waking moment of the day.

I know others who have gone through painful experiences understand that when pain is constant and ongoing, there's no escape. One of the mental cues and strategies I used to help me during my previous traumas was to look up at the clock for hope. I knew as the clock kept moving, my hip would eventually drop into place and the steel rod could be removed from my leg. The force of the traction was so strong that it pulled my entire body toward the bottom of the bed, creating a tug-of-war between the traction pulling on my knee and me trying to move back up higher in the bed. Honestly, this felt like what I would imagine if a large alligator clamped down on your leg and was trying to pull it off your body. I was utterly miserable with pain every waking moment, and my wife bore the brunt of my discomfort. Every 20-30 minutes, I would be pulled to the bottom of the bed, and I would try to sit up and move back to the top of the bed, pulling against the traction that was pulling on my leg.

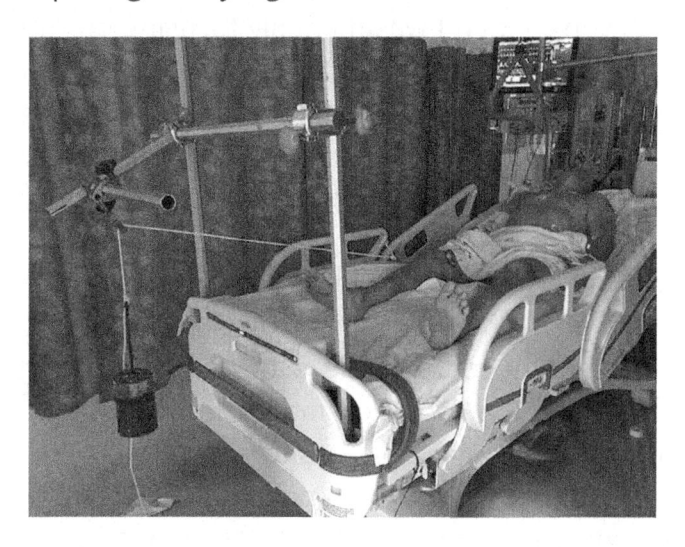

I remember lying in bed with the door open to the hallway when I recognized someone walking by. They noticed me as well, and from just a few seconds of observing me, they could see the sheer pain I was in, making it clear that it was not a good time to visit. I could see their steps change direction from turning toward my room to abruptly continuing down the hall. After this, I asked my wife to please get up and close the door; I didn't want to see anybody, talk to anyone, or have anyone see me in this condition. The reality is there are times in life when there's no escape from pain, no matter what you do or what medication you take, suffering happens. It was one of those times. Only time would end the suffering.

It took a couple of days of traction before my hip finally settled back into place where it should be. There was both good news and bad news. The good news was that once my hip had returned to its proper location, I could have the steel rod and traction apparatus removed from my leg, finally bringing an end to the tug-of-war I had endured over the last few days. The bad news was I was informed the removal of the rod would be more painful than its insertion. I didn't think this would be possible.

As the procedure began, they unhooked the traction cables, which was an immense relief. The continuing pulling force on my leg was instantly gone. The next step, which I dreaded, was the removal of the steel rod. The process involved using a drill to back the rod out of the hole. As they started to unscrew and pull out the rod, I was surprised by the resistance I felt. It seemed in the short time the rod had been in my body; my muscle and other tissues had grown attached to it. As the rod was being removed, I experienced a sensation of tissue and muscle being torn away from the bar. The resistance caused the procedure to take much longer than putting the rod in.

During the removal, I found it impossible to mentally escape the pain, using the strategy that had helped me many times before. My anxiety was too high to allow any relaxation or mental diversion. So, I did exactly what I had to: I just suffered through it. I clenched my fists and jaws and kept waiting to feel the pin exit my leg and the procedure end. I got to the point where I was just wincing and groaning due to the pain. I kept telling myself, "It will be over soon; just a little bit longer." Time seemed to stop during this inopportune time. Finally, in an instant, the pain stopped. A feeling of joy and a sense of accomplishment washed over me. It is amazing how you can go from one extreme to another in seconds. This also marked the time when my release from the hospital would soon follow.

Once I was released from the hospital and back home, my next set of challenges awaited me. I knew another long-term rehabilitation was ahead of me due to the multiple pelvic fractures. I would not be allowed to bear any weight for two months. During these two months, I was introduced to a wheelchair, followed by a walker and then crutches. This rehabilitation was different from my previous experiences because I was far more dependent on others for help. I needed assistance with bathing, using the bathroom, getting dressed and doing other daily tasks due to my lack of mobility. Being so reliant on others made me angry. I believe my anger stemmed not just from dependency, but from the continuous discomfort I was in.

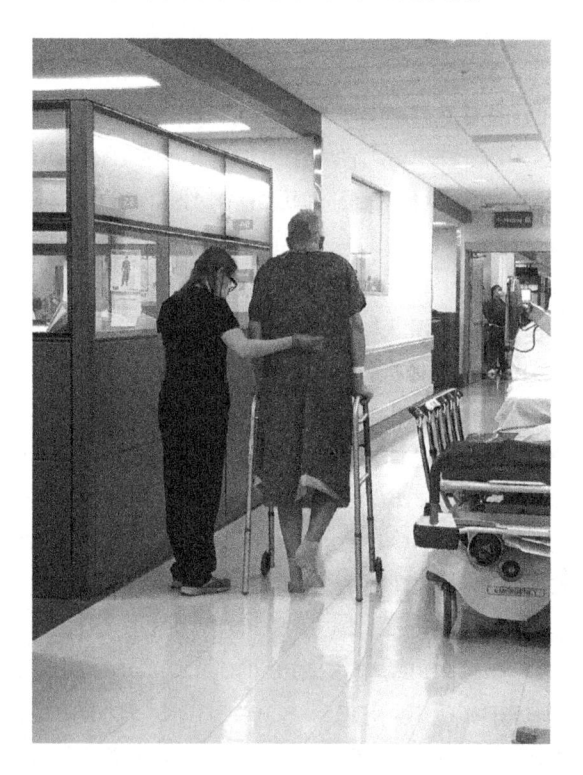

I was being introduced to things I never thought I would need for another 30-plus years. My daily routine now included using a shower chair and safety handles installed in the shower. I also made use of a portable frame and toilet seat that fit over the toilet because it was impossible for me to bend down far enough to sit on the commode. My previous rehabs involved reliance on others but not for as long as this situation was going to last. The other rehabs also didn't require the use of so many assistive devices. It is very humbling to find yourself in need of these items when you typically wouldn't need any until the later years in life.

The journey through rehabilitation was fraught with numerous challenges. I eventually transitioned from the wheelchair to the walker to crutches. I was not prepared for the physical therapy walking. The realization that I needed assistance in relearning such a fundamental skill didn't initially sink in. At no point did I ever think walking would be necessary to relearn. After spending two months without bearing any weight, it was time to walk without any assistance.

I'll never forget the first time I was instructed to take a step during rehab. Positioned between parallel bars, I gripped them tightly with both hands, keeping the weight off my legs. The therapist encouraged me to gradually let the weight back on my legs by releasing my arms and taking a step. Despite my brain commanding my leg to move, my body simply wouldn't comply. Fear surged through me, and my anxiety skyrocketed as I wondered why my body wasn't responding. I never considered this would be the response of my brain and body after getting rid of crutches. I was able to use one crutch to walk for the previous week and thought the transition to not using it would be simple. I wasn't prepared for how wrong I was. It was like my brain rebelled and wouldn't allow my leg to take a step.

Once I managed to calm down, I focused intently on the physical therapist's instructions. Gradually, I was able to ease off the bars and stand without supporting my weight. Initially, I had to take steps while gripping the bars. Each session brought incremental progress, and eventually, I could take steps without any support. The next adjustment was teaching my right side I didn't have to favor it to walk. Pelvis injuries, I was told, go through this progression. It wasn't painful, but it was mentally exhausting. I felt it was my brain not trusting me to take a step, anticipating pain. The natural tendency was to favor the leg by not allowing all the weight to transfer to my injured side. Through regular practice, I got better and better, eventually getting my normal walking gait back. The harsh reality of how long it would take for a full recovery slapped me in the face. It was a familiar road; I knew how to navigate physical pain, but this type of mental struggle with my mind was totally new.

Even though my injuries brought me unimaginable pain and mental anguish, there were some positive outcomes. One positive outcome is that when you go through an extended rehabilitation, you get a feeling of accomplishment. There is a relief knowing that the hard part of the ordeal is behind you. It does provide confidence in moving forward. For instance, whatever painful moments await me in the future, it's hard to believe they could compare with what I have already experienced. Also, experiencing incidents so painful gives you hope for the rest of your recovery because mentally, you can tell yourself you've made it through the worst part.

Breaking the recovery down into segmented goals is a strategy that worked for me. After getting through the internal bleeding stress, I was then able to focus on the hip/traction. Once I made it through this, I was able to focus on adjusting to life with assistance, and finally, I was able to focus on rehabilitation to walk. After all these steps were completed, I turned my attention to improving my overall health and started the process of getting back in shape. By breaking recovery down into segments, it minimizes the potential of being overwhelmed. I learned it was manageable to focus on one aspect at a time.

Another positive I noticed after my third traumatic event is that I became more empathetic and compassionate about what others are going through. You realize when you're in the hospital that there are people filling every room on every floor, and they all have their stories of pain. It is a great reminder that you are not the only person facing difficult challenges. Those of us who are no strangers to pain also realize there are people going through situations that are just as bad or worse than what you are going through. Being humbled allows you to find the good in terrible times. Dealing with pain takes a mindset of determination and focus. Knowing what to focus on and when is how you get through each day and ultimately say goodbye to pain. Pain is a good teacher.

8
A Rehabilitation in the Gym & Life

I pulled into the parking space and put my truck in park. I reached across the seat and grabbed my crutches, lying on the passenger side from the floor to the top of the seat. I opened the door, put the crutch down and gently lowered myself to the ground. I tried to park close to the door to limit the distance I would have to maneuver with my crutches. As I approached the door, someone else who was going in held the door open. As I entered, I walked up to the desk and handed my card to officially check in. I then made my way over to my first exercise machine, sat down and started my workout. This was the first day that I went to Planet Fitness during my rehab after my 2020 accident.

I joined Planet Fitness to take advantage of their variety of machines, which allowed me to work on my overall fitness. I started going there three times a week. When I first began visiting Planet Fitness, I was still on crutches—about six weeks into my recovery. To this day, I can't recall seeing anyone else working out who was on crutches. Reflecting, the thought of not going never even crossed my mind. After a decade of three traumatic events and long rehabilitations, I was in familiar territory. I think I was made for this, my life as an athlete, Physical Education & Health teacher and a track/cross country coach provided me with a great foundation of understanding rehabilitation and mental focus it takes. Daily rehabilitation was now a part of my life and who I was. It became as natural a part of my life as going to work.

After my second serious cycling accident, I decided to add an exercise room to the basement to support my recovery. My family was one hundred percent behind this investment. They preferred I get on my NordicTrack bike and eliminate the chance of a third accident. I was totally focused on improving my overall fitness; this time it included muscular strength by lifting weights. I wasn't ready mentally or emotionally to focus on cycling or getting back on the bike. I was in my element working out and confident I could set a new goal to get my muscular strength to a level my body hadn't reached in several years.

The mental and emotional struggles stemming from the three traumatic events were the main struggles I was facing. I couldn't allow myself to think about riding out on the roads due to the mental trauma. I hoped to get back on the bike eventually, but it was too much for me now. I had a fear I would need to overcome before getting back on the bike. Not working out wasn't an option for me; I still needed the physical exertion for my mental health. I still needed a goal to focus on and to measure progress. Lifting weights and concentrating on total body fitness was my answer.

I continued to grapple with bouts of depression and overwhelming emotions, often feeling paralyzed and unwilling to do anything. This, to me, was one of the most difficult aspects of recovering from trauma. If you're not careful, you can become so overwhelmed that you feel stuck. You don't want to get up, you don't want to work out, you don't want to talk to anybody; you're just fed up. The physical and emotional pain has a way of gradually wearing you down. It's a vicious cycle that you're constantly battling against. Even though I should be considered an expert on rehabilitation, it is always a struggle mentally facing depression. Chronic pain is one of the culprits which begins slowly wearing me down over time. Since 2010, I have never had a day without a part of my body aching. I have no delusions that I will one day be pain-free. My life will include daily reminders of what my body has gone through. In a similar fashion, it is not realistic for me to think the emotional impact will gradually disappear. Rehabilitation of my body and life will be an ongoing process for the remainder of my days.

Searching for new ways to stay motivated was very important for me in dealing with trauma. One of the new strategies I used to help me stay motivated was getting a tattoo on my forearm. The tattoo I chose was a picture of a cyclist on a bike with the word "resilience" written underneath it. I like the fact that the tattoo is always there, a daily reminder of how resilient I have been throughout my life. This proved to be even more effective than I thought it would be when I first came up with the idea. Any time I would find myself slipping into negative thoughts or being overwhelmed, it was easy to glance down at my forearm and remember everything that I had accomplished. It became a badge of honor, something I could be proud of.

Another benefit of getting a tattoo is that it became a conversation piece. Others would notice it and then ask me about its meaning. I could tell my story of what I survived. Being able to share my story with others was great therapy for me. This also became part of my presentation when I spoke. I was able to tell my story about my tattoo when I spoke during the 2022 Kentucky AmeriCorps Accelerator Conference. The tattoo was a great prop for a presentation, and I never had to worry about forgetting it or leaving it at home. The tattoo was one of the most powerful strategies I have used for my mental and emotional health. I look at it multiple times every day. Sometimes I look at it intentionally as positive reinforcement, whereas other times I find myself being drawn to it while performing everyday tasks.

In 2022, something else happened that took my rehabilitation from the gym to the real world. During late July of that year, there was massive flooding in eastern Kentucky. My mother-in-law, who lived in eastern Kentucky, lost everything, including the house she was living in, to the flood. Unfortunately, this was not the first time this had ever happened. To make matters worse, her health was declining due to dementia. My wife and her family had the goal of trying to fix the house and get her back into her home as soon as possible before her health declined so much that she would not be able to be there. Her mother had lived in this location for over sixty years. Fortunately, my job focuses on serving eastern Kentucky schools in this region through a national program. Our company mission was serving Appalachia, so they were willing to provide resources such as time and allow me to work over there as much as possible.

Starting in July 2022, I had a brand-new focus, which was to help get my mother-in-law's house put back together. I had a great deal of support from my local church, which provided me with funds for the project. I also had volunteers who would come and help me do the work. I spent every weekend and many days during the week for the following three-plus months helping put her house back together. I was not spending a lot of time at the gym, but I was spending a great deal of time, energy and effort putting the house back together. I was fortunate that my focus the previous two years had been to improve my muscular strength. The house had to be stripped down to its wooden wall studs and down to the subfloor to be totally cleaned, disinfected and then rebuilt. I was involved in every aspect of the rebuild. Just driving and getting the supplies loaded and unloaded was a major undertaking. I did most of this part on my own and spent many hours alone rebuilding her house. During this process, it seemed to move at a snail's pace, and I wondered if we were ever going to get the house complete so she could live in it. One of the lessons I learned through my multiple traumas was not to get overwhelmed; just keep moving and focus on one segment at a time. Do whatever you can at that moment to make progress. I was mentally prepared for this.

It was a minor miracle, but only through the help and donations of others were we able to complete the home, get it fully refurnished and have her moved back in by the end of October. This project became a positive distraction for me, allowing me to focus on something meaningful and gain personal growth by serving others. I worked so hard that I was physically exhausted by the end of each day. I was proud my focus never wavered, no matter how tired I was. This was the exact mental focus that got me through three traumatic events.

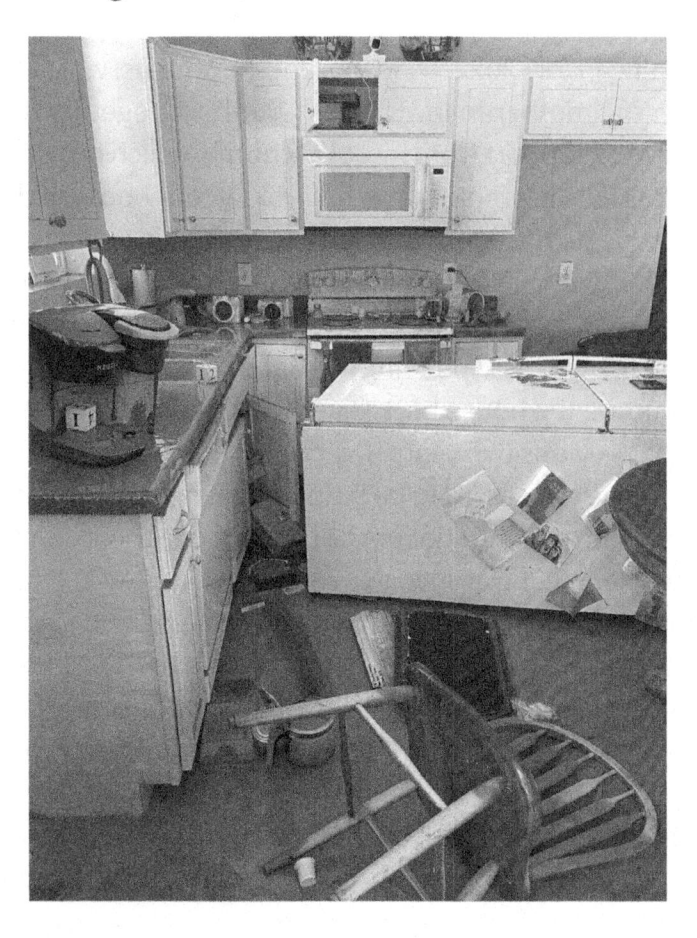

A Rehabilitation in the Gym & Life | 75

In the past, I wouldn't have had the confidence to undertake such a massive task. My ability to accomplish this was largely due to a shift in mindset following my first traumatic accident. I was no longer intimidated by the prospect of trying new things or dedicating time to learning new skills. Over the years, I became proficient in handy work and familiar with various tools. Nothing seemed intimidating; I viewed things totally differently. My traumatic experiences prepared me to be able to rebuild a house. It wasn't so much about the drive to do it but mental confidence and mindset. I was even more prepared to help with the rebuild after the flood because, in 2016, we bought a small lake house and completely gutted and renovated it. I personally did a significant amount of work and assisted throughout the entire rebuilding process. This was something prior to 2010 I would never have attempted. These traumatic experiences transformed my mindset by instilling confidence, eliminating fear and fostering a willingness to explore new ventures. Nothing seemed too hard when compared to what I have endured physically and mentally. The destruction of the flood also demonstrated I was a fortunate person and the least I could do was my part.

There were always milestones during rehab in the gym and in real life which provided positive reinforcement. By searching for ways to stay active and to grow personally, I was able to combat the negative impacts of trauma. There is such a fine line between personal growth and being overwhelmed and unable to move. Overcoming trauma allows you to open your mind to new opportunities. Utilizing your trauma in good ways takes awareness, intention and focus. These are all things that will help you get through trauma.

I could generate a long list of new skills and small accomplishments I have made after experiencing my first trauma.

This list was added to after each of my life-changing events. There are lessons to be learned, but you must look for them and seek them out. This is what I am referring to when I say you "have to keep moving, or you will become paralyzed." Moving mentally and physically will continue your rehab of body and life. I am thankful I have developed confidence and skills which I did not have prior to 2010. Getting involved in the rebuilding of my mother-in-law's house was a long-term distraction from my trauma and physical effects. I realized I could make a difference. I could take it one day at a time and make progress. The mindset of determination under overwhelming circumstances is something I am experienced at due to my traumatic experiences. I was prepared to make a difference.

I have heard several times about Thomas Edison's perseverance, one of the most prolific inventors in history, is a quintessential example of perseverance after repeated failures. Edison's journey to invent the electric light bulb was fraught with obstacles and setbacks. He is famously quoted as saying, "I have not failed. I've just found 10,000 ways that won't work." This mindset epitomized Edison's relentless determination to succeed despite numerous disappointments.

In the late 1870s, Edison embarked on the arduous task of developing a practical and affordable electric light bulb. He tested thousands of different materials for the filament, experiencing failure after failure. Each unsuccessful attempt provided him with valuable insights and brought him one step closer to success. Finally, in 1879, Edison discovered that a carbonized bamboo filament could burn for over 1,200 hours, leading to the creation of a commercially viable light bulb. This breakthrough not only revolutionized lighting but also laid the foundation for the modern electric utility industry.

Edison's story is a testament to the power of perseverance. Despite encountering countless failures, he remained undeterred and continued to innovate. His ability to learn from mistakes and persist in the face of adversity serves as an inspiration to many, demonstrating that success is often the result of relentless determination and a refusal to give up.

9
Mothers Gifts & Finding Purpose

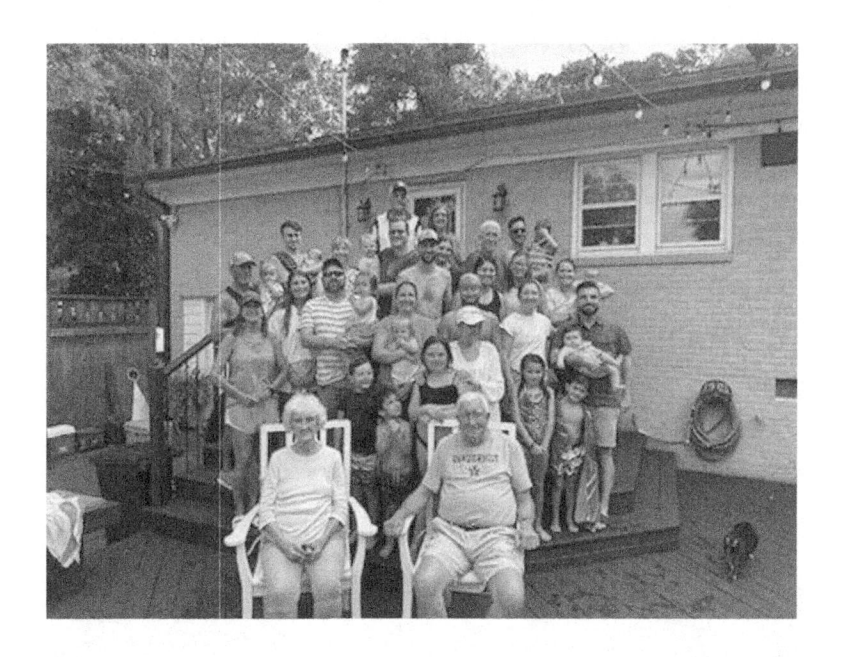

During my freshman year in college, I lived in a dorm, and to make a phone call, I had to walk out into the hallway and use one of the two rotary phones at each end of the hallway. It was November 1983. I remember picking up the phone and calling home. Mom answered, and I began to tell her that college was too difficult for me and that I didn't think I could do the work. I was prepared and told her all the reasons I didn't belong in college.

As mothers do so well, she listened to every word and never interrupted me throughout my litany of reasons. Finally, there was silence, and I will never forget her words, which came across the phone line: "Well, why don't you stay there another month and give it your best? At the end of the semester, when you come home, you can decide then if you want to go back."

Mothers just know what to say to get the outcome they know is best. I finished the semester, passed my classes and returned to the college where I would graduate four years later. This was one of the best gifts I ever received from Mom. Throughout life, even as adults, mothers and mothers-in-law have many lessons for us to learn.

Shortly after my mother-in-law moved back into her home after the flood in 2022, her health started to deteriorate. She had only been living in her remodeled home for a little over two weeks when she suffered a stroke. She would not be able to return to the home we worked so hard to prepare. In January 2023, my mother's health also started to decline. Life had entered a new, challenging chapter for my family. My mother-in-law passed away in the spring of 2023, and shortly thereafter, my mother was diagnosed with terminal kidney disease.

Going through the experience of losing my mother-in-law made it painfully clear to me that the nature of life can be profoundly traumatic. As I navigated this period of loss, I began to see similarities between these experiences and other traumatic events I had faced. It was a reminder of the fragility and unpredictability of life. I also noticed how resilience played a big part in getting through these difficult times. Having the proper mindset is the foundation for resilience.

As we learned more about my mother's terminal illness, my daughter and niece decided to host a family reunion in July that would bring everyone together one more time with Mom. It wasn't known whether Mom would still be with us for Christmas, when annually we would all gather. The July gathering was kind of a Christmas in July. Every sibling, every grandchild and every great-grandchild made the event. This was a testament to how Mom taught us the value of family and what she meant to all of us. There were over thirty of us who traveled from out of state.

From the July family reunion until September 23, 2023, the day my mother passed, I spent a great deal of time in Mississippi. During her final weeks, my sisters and I were able to be with Mom while she was in the hospital. We were so thankful for this time and the memories we were able to make with her up until her final days. During her last month of life, aside from the last week or so, she was coherent, sharp and kept her sense of humor. I found joy just sitting and watching her interact with my sisters. Their relationship was special, just as mine was with her, but in a totally different way. She represented what the epitome of mother and daughter relationships should be. One of her final gifts was demonstrating how to use your last days. I never saw her down, I never heard her complain; there was only love. I couldn't help but see the value she brought to her last days.

I spent a lot of time reflecting on how difficult life is during this period, as my wife and I would be losing our mothers just months apart. I started wondering, what were some of the things I could do to help me, and others deal with the impending loss of Mom? The past several years of my life, I was accustomed to finding ways to overcome physical and emotional trauma. It was natural for me to apply the same problem-solving mindset to the pain of losing my mother. The emotional pain was just as severe during this time as the multiple traumas I had endured. I wanted the remaining time I had with Mom to be meaningful. I came up with a plan and decided to focus on what I could do to support my father and my sisters during Mom's last days and after she passed. I had the ability to focus on their needs and help them deal with the grief. I had no idea how powerful this approach would be in helping me deal with her loss. I was able to find value, meaning and worth during a time of loss by shifting the focus from grief to helping others.

One of the first things I decided to do was plan the meaningful actions I could take while Mom was still alive. First was to make sure I told her I loved her every night before leaving. I knew there would be a limited number of opportunities to do this. One day, while Mom was still alert and aware, I bent down and whispered in her ear, "Mom, I'm going to write a book." She was the first person I shared this goal with. I had been contemplating writing a book for several years. By telling her, I knew it would hold me accountable and make it happen. There was no way I was going to let her down by not following through with what I told her. She had given me so many gifts throughout life; it was a small way I could repay her. My first book would always be associated with my promise to her. As fate would have it, a few days later I was getting ready to leave, and I bent down and told her I loved her as I did each night. On this night, she looked at me and said, "My Robbie." These would be the last words she would say.

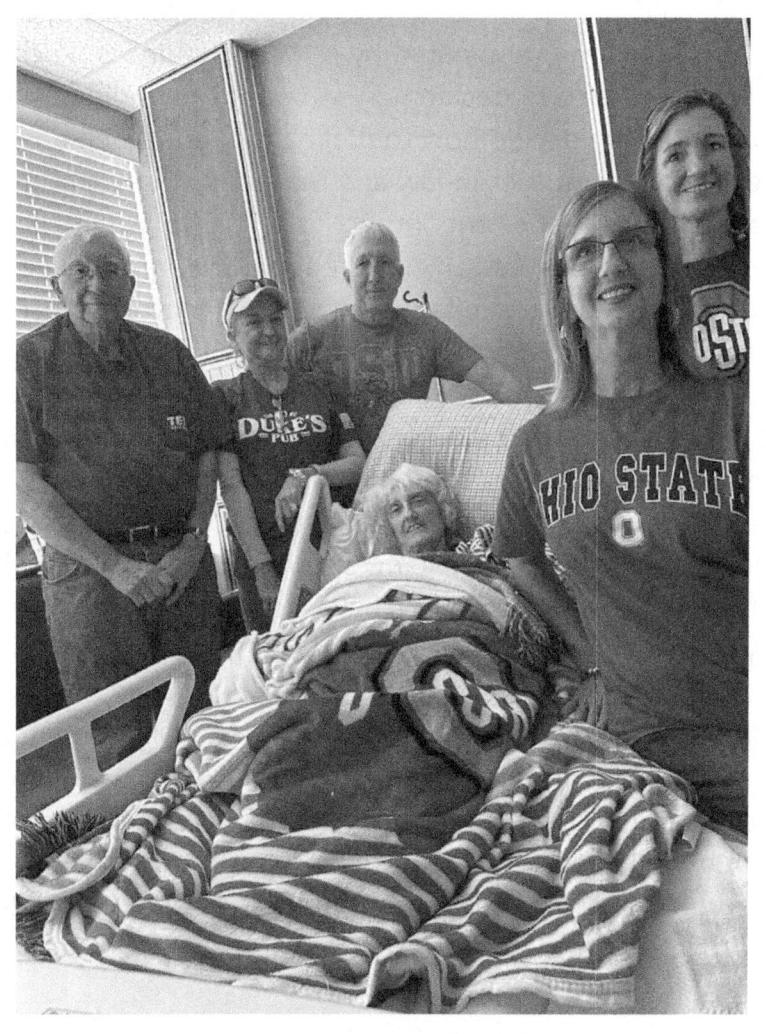

Going through the process of losing Mom reaffirmed my need to write a book and share what I have learned through so many different types of traumas. I started seeing connections with loss and traumatic events I experienced. My understanding of trauma was evolving. Emotionally dealing with loss presents challenges like other types of traumatic events. I immediately saw the mindset to focus on one segment at a time was useful in dealing with both trauma and loss. I also started to see how during both challenging times, personal growth could be an outcome. The period during loss doesn't have to be a time dominated by grief and sadness. Each of us has the choice to decide how we want to handle periods of loss. We can decide how to make time more meaningful. The loss of my mother-in-law and mother just months apart allowed me to notice the impact loss has on family. If the timing of their loss was any different, I don't know if I would have connected the similarities. This was another gift from our mothers, which I planned on sharing.

As I started to see the role resilience can play in everyday life, it was like a whole new world opened up. I learned from spending time with my mother that resilience can also play a role in personal growth and becoming a better person. As I focused on how I could help my sisters and father during this difficult time, it allowed me to have a purpose and a positive way to deal with loss. The help you give others during times like this doesn't have to be major acts of kindness and empathy. Small gestures and actions are just as powerful. I remember when my sister, father and I were meeting with the hospice director to officially have Mom moved there; it was a very emotional time. All three of us had lumps in our throats as the director went over papers. After finishing going over the forms, he needed signatures. Noticing how upset my sister and father were at this moment, I volunteered to sign the forms. If I were not focusing on helping others, this would not have happened. I would have assumed Dad should sign them and waited for him. Instead, I acted because I was thinking about him and my sister.

Another example of a small gesture demonstrating love and compassion was the day we were told Mom's ashes were ready to be picked up. My father asked my sister to take care of this, and I decided right away I would not allow her to do this alone. It would be another difficult moment I could make better just by going along. I will give Mom the credit for helping me link the benefits of resiliency during times of loss by focusing on serving others. A person must be resilient to put their emotions of loss and sadness aside in order to help others deal with loss. I also will give her the credit for knowing when you put others' needs first, you get rewarded just as much as those you serve. Isn't that what mothers do?

My next major focus after Mom passed on September 23, 2023, was putting my father's needs first by preparing our house in West Virginia so he could live there. Like 2022, after the Eastern Kentucky floods, I would now be spending my weekends in West Virginia, building a new room on the house and adding electricity, water and sewage. Our house in West Virginia originally belonged to my grandfather and became Dad's after his passing. This is near where Dad spent a great deal of his childhood, and it's a place where he truly loves to be, and his support system of friends is there. The old off-the-grid farm is a place he and I have always visited since the time I was 3-4 years old. As a matter of fact, Dad and I had a tradition of spending Thanksgiving in West Virginia deer hunting from the time I was old enough to hunt through to the present (44 years). I had no doubt when Mom passed where he would want to live and spend most of his time.

Starting in October 2023, I had already contacted the electric company and started the ball rolling to schedule having electricity run to our house in WV. The closest electric access was half a mile away. The time frame for completion for electricity was set for April, 2024. This meant I needed to have a new addition consisting of a kitchen and bathroom completed by April. I was able to get things organized and started building the addition in January 2024. Most of my weekends were spent working on the addition. Due to the invaluable help of two friends, I was able to complete the addition, get the electric, water and septic systems installed and hooked up. We finally moved Dad in by the first week of May 2024.

Mothers Gifts & Finding Purpose | 87

Upon completing the project, I realized that the past two years had felt like an extended period of crisis and construction. My commitment to honoring my mother's memory by creating something positive out of her passing provided a purpose I needed. This purpose I gained not only allowed my father to reside where he needed to be, but it also gave me a great deal of pride in making it possible for Dad to move to West Virginia. I was able to channel my grief into meaningful action and personal growth.

My search for purpose in my life started during my recovery after my 2020 accident. I started thinking about all the challenges that I had faced over the past ten years. Many friends and family members made statements to me like: "You must be like a cat and have nine lives," "God isn't finished with you yet," and "It wasn't your time," just to name a few. These comments started me searching for how I could find purpose from my traumatic experiences. I was determined to make something positive out of the traumatic events and pain I had experienced for over a decade.

One of my first thoughts concerning finding purpose was to share my experiences by speaking to others. Unlike many people, I always enjoyed speaking in front of groups. During my years of coaching track and field and cross country, I had the privilege to speak at a handful of coaches' clinics. I found that speaking about something I was passionate about to interested listeners was natural. I could envision doing the same thing concerning resilience and overcoming trauma. The strong urge to share my story only grew stronger through the loss of my mother and mother-in-law.

It wasn't long after my 2020 accident that I started researching how to write a book. I was in the middle of playing mental tennis, wondering: Is speaking where I need to focus, or should I write a book? There was never a question of whether I was going to speak or write about my experiences. It was a matter of when and how. I knew at this time that resilience and overcoming trauma were the two themes constantly on my mind. I felt a certain calling to write about these two interconnected things. The past fifteen years of my life could be narrowed down to resilience and overcoming trauma.

Years ago, after the hit-and-run accident in 2010, I sat down and penned my thoughts about the incident. I described in detail what happened and every emotion I experienced. Then, my writing was more for self-healing than for teaching. I never had a thought about writing a book about my experience. My focus was unpacking the emotional baggage. Searching for meaning and purpose was still a few traumatic events away.

Traumatic events have a way of making you feel lonely. You are the one living with the relentless physical and emotional pain—there is no respite. Each person experiencing trauma can find meaning and purpose in life by how they respond. I have searched for meaning, value and purpose in my life because of the succession of traumatic events I have experienced. I know there must be a way I can use my traumatic experiences to help others deal with theirs. After each trauma, my desire for finding meaning and purpose increased. I refused to believe there wasn't a valuable purpose behind the agony, pain and suffering I endured.

If I was ever going to be able to put all my experiences together and find meaning and purpose, it would be soon and due to a broken heart.

10
Broken Heart

I started the weed eater and began cutting the weeds along the edge of the field. it was a steep bank three or four feet high that ended at the edge of the gravel road. I was starting the weed eating around the front meadow across from our house in West Virginia. The sun was bright and warm, and it didn't take long for sweat to start running down the side of my face.

I was dressed appropriately for cutting thick weeds, wearing boots, gloves, goggles, a hat and a long-sleeved shirt. I learned to wear the proper gear while working for the Forestry Department while in college. I have done this same annual weed eating each April or May for the past 25-30 years. The first time cutting the weeds is always the most difficult and takes the most amount of time. I knew I would be weed eating for most of the day. Typically, it would take five full tanks of gas to complete the weed eating along the edges of our property. Over the years, I learned to enjoy the sweat eventually soaking through my pants and shirt because when the weed eating was completed, there wasn't a more beautiful place than our house nestled between mountains with beautiful, manicured fields along streams in West Virginia.

Today, something was not right. Unlike all the previous weed-eating sessions of years past, I turned off the weed eater. I was just starting my second tank of the day, and I was exhausted. I walked with the weed eater held by the strap across my shoulder toward the front porch. I was feeling a little light-headed as I made my way to the porch. I took the weed eater off my shoulder and sat down on the edge of the porch. This was strange; I felt like all my energy was gone. I sat there wondering why this day and this time was different from any other time. Was I coming down with a bug? All I knew was that as soon as I cooled off, I was going to change clothes and lie down. I started to ask, was 59 that much different than 58? I was never tired after one tank of weed eating, let alone exhausted. This was one of the first indicators of what 2024 would bring.

During May 2024, I was hopeful that some normalcy would return to my life. I eagerly anticipated getting back to work, focusing solely on my job without the added stress of family and construction issues. Dad had moved into the house in West

Virginia, and I was ready to start mowing and weed eating there for the season. I looked forward to my time of working and sweating in the mountains.

However, throughout the spring and early summer, I sensed that something was off with my health. Having dealt with numerous health challenges over the past 14 years, I was confident in my ability to recognize when things weren't right. I found myself unusually tired and craving sleep far more than usual. Given the past two years of relentless stress, it was logical to attribute my exhaustion to both physical and emotional fatigue.

Taking a proactive approach, I ensured that I scheduled an appointment and visited the doctor. The initial plan was to run blood tests to determine if we could identify any underlying issues. When all my lab results came back, they were within the normal range. The next step was to see if I would start feeling better over the following 2-3 weeks by just eating and sleeping better, which weren't ever an issue.

As time passed and my condition remained unchanged after 3 weeks, my doctor referred me to a cardiologist as a precaution to see if any issues were going on with my heart. I was scheduled for a series of tests, including a stress test, an EKG and an ultrasound of my heart. After waiting a few more weeks for my appointment, I finally went and completed all the tests. I was told the cardiologist would look at my test results and call me in a day or two. The next day I waited for the phone to ring; I was eager to find out if there was something wrong because my energy and stamina were very low. I needed to know if there was a reason for this, rather than just getting old. A part of me almost hoped that something would be found, just to validate that I wasn't imagining the problem.

The phone finally rang late in the afternoon, and the doctor told me the results came back showing no issues with my heart.

He did say, based on my symptoms, he would schedule a heart catheterization several weeks later if my symptoms remained unchanged. Consequently, I was booked for a heart cath procedure to take place later in August.

During July, I continued to experience extreme fatigue. Whenever I exert significant energy, such as when using a weed eater, walking up the trail from my dock, or moving furniture, I would become dizzy and need to sit down to recuperate. Over the past couple of months, I performed all three of these activities multiple times with the same result. As soon as I exerted a good amount of energy, I was literally done until I caught my breath and took a break for a few minutes. On Wednesday, July 24, after walking up the steep trail from our dock, I had to stop and catch my breath three times. I noticed my heart rate skyrocketed after walking up the trail not even a fourth of the way. At no time since walking up and down this trail for the past eight years had I ever had to stop and rest. I always took pride in being in good cardiovascular shape. This time was vastly different; I began to develop pain above my upper teeth in my gums and jaw. My heart was pounding, and my breathing was elevated and now my gums/roof of my mouth were throbbing with intense pain. I continued up the trail, stopping and resting another two or three times until I stepped into the backyard and immediately sat down in a chair beside our fire pit. I sat there for ten minutes, resting and getting my heart rate down so I could recover and go up the steps onto the deck and into the house.

Later that evening, the pain in my gums and the roof of my mouth never eased up. I texted my primary care physician to inform him that I was experiencing severe jaw pain and had no idea what was going on. I informed him of my trip up the trail and how everything started. It was already nine o'clock or so in the evening. He advised me to call my cardiologist first thing in the morning. So, the next morning at 9:00 a.m., I called the cardiologist and told the receptionist what I was experiencing. As soon as I mentioned my jaws and the roof of my mouth were hurting a great deal, she interrupted and told me, "Get to the emergency room now." It could be a sign of a heart attack.

My wife was getting ready for work in the bathroom, and I told her about my call and the urgency to get to the ER at once. After the shock wore off, we both got ready and headed to the emergency room. It was a Thursday morning, and as soon as I arrived at the ER, I was quickly taken back to a room and hooked up to a heart monitor and IV. This wasn't the start to the morning I expected. They did blood work and EKGs and decided to admit me overnight and move up my heart cath and do it Friday morning. At this point, my wife and I were both quite anxious and still in a little shock about how fast things moved on this day. Neither of us ever imagined I would have an issue with my heart; it seemed impossible to me. The more I started thinking about the potential of a heart issue, the more disbelief I felt.

The next morning, I was prepped and ready for the procedure. I had no idea what to expect. My wife was allowed to accompany me and the two nurses as they wheeled me down to the floor where the procedure would take place. As we reached a certain point, the nurses paused and instructed my wife, "Now is the time you can give him a kiss and tell him you will see him when he gets back to the room." So, she gave me a kiss and told me she would see me soon. She was ushered into a surgery waiting room close to the room where the procedure was taking place.

As she walked away, I couldn't help but think about the three previous times in my life when I had to say goodbye to my wife, not knowing if I would ever see her or anyone else again. Although heart catheterizations are typically routine, the other three instances were serious and potentially life-threatening. Just the act of saying goodbye and then being rolled on a hospital bed away from her brought back some of the fear and anxiety I'd felt after my previous traumatic events. A rush of fear and panic washed over me as I was in the surgery room getting ready for the procedure. I tried to talk myself down by focusing on the fact that the procedure is typically low risk, and I will be fine. There was just something about a potential heart issue that made this event different.

I was pleased to wake up after the procedure and find myself back in my room. The heart catheterization revealed that I had a 90 percent blockage in the main artery of my heart, famously known as the "widow maker." Additionally, they discovered another blockage and placed stents to address both issues.

My initial reaction was one of validation; I wasn't imagining things when I felt something was off over the past four to five months. My second thought was a mix of astonishment and gratitude, wondering how I had managed to survive given the numerous strenuous activities I had engaged in during those months. I could have easily had a massive heart attack and never made it to a hospital. It was an eye-opening experience; one my wife and I were still having difficulty processing the facts.

I was ready to be discharged on Saturday. After being discharged, I returned home on Saturday to begin my recovery. I woke up Sunday morning, and I still didn't feel well. I was under the impression that after the stent, I would feel better almost immediately. By Sunday evening, I was experiencing pulsating chest pains. These pains weren't intense, but they bothered me mentally because they were new. I didn't know what I should or shouldn't feel. I texted my cardiologist's assistant that night to inform her of my symptoms. She advised me to go back to the emergency room and get it checked right away. There is a certain seriousness when dealing with the heart, as I have learned over the past few days. So, we loaded up and made the trip to the emergency room.

Sunday night at the emergency room, they decided to admit me for further tests to ensure everything was alright. An echocardiogram was scheduled for Monday. Late Monday morning, they came and picked me up to roll me down for the echocardiogram. The procedure didn't take long, and within a few hours, we had the results. Thankfully, the results came back good. I was discharged on Monday and returned home to restart my recovery again.

During my week at home, the seriousness of my condition weighed heavily on my mind. Each time a friend or family member called to check on me, they always remarked on how amazing it was that I had been through so much. After hearing similar communications over and over, I started feeling guilty for not starting the book I promised Mom I would write. This had to be the final wake-up call to get it done.

The past fourteen years of my life have been anything but simple, especially concerning my health issues. After a period of recovery, I returned to work, hoping for a semblance of normalcy. All of this was new to me. I didn't know how heart recovery went. I wasn't sure how I was supposed to feel. This was one rehab I didn't understand like the others I had been through.

A few weeks later, on August 14th, I experienced a familiar pain in my jaw as I walked up the trail from the dock. This pain was strikingly like what had initially sent me to the hospital. Why was I experiencing this pain again? I was anxious, and I texted my cardiologist's assistant. It was nice feeling comfortable to call and ask her questions. She promptly instructed me to go to the ER. This would be my third trip to the hospital. I wondered if I was overreacting. I was tired of trips to the hospital.

Just like my previous visits, I went to the ER, and I was admitted. The medical team performed an echocardiogram, an ultrasound and blood tests to check my troponin levels. Although my levels were elevated, this could be considered normal due to the heart cath procedure I had undergone a few weeks earlier. I learned troponin is present when the heart has been stressed or damaged. The other tests were inconclusive, but the doctors still had some concern, and the decision was made to perform another heart catheterization. This entire experience was beginning to feel like a real-life version of Groundhog Day. I was back in the hospital, wondering if I was a hypochondriac or if my heart had serious issues. Either way, it was not comforting.

I went through the same routine: My bed was rolled down the hall to the procedure room, and I said goodbye to my wife, which was not as bad as the last time, but still gave me pause. I was in the surgery room and underwent the procedure. I was awake while on the way back to my room. When I returned, my wife and I were alone, and she informed me that they had inserted a third stent.

As I lay in the bed, I mentioned to my wife that I was starting to feel nauseous. The moment those words left my mouth, my brain sent me into panic mode. I can't describe the sensation other than my brain knowing something was very wrong. The next second, I vividly remember pressing the emergency red button on my bed for the nursing station. It was as if my brain made the decision and instructed my body to complete the action. It didn't feel like a conscious decision from me. My wife, noticing my distress, asked me a question from across the room where she was sitting. I didn't respond. Concerned, she got up, walked over to the bed, touched my arm and spoke to me. Although my eyes were open, there was no reaction from me.

At this point, she stepped out into the hall and urgently summoned help from the hallway. The nurses' station had received the emergency call I had made and was already heading toward my room. When the nurse entered my room, my blood pressure had plummeted, causing warning signals to go off. The Rapid Response Team emergency signal was activated by the nurse. My next memory was of my room being filled with people, and a female doctor was right in my face, repeatedly urging, "Stay with me! Stay with me!"

I could see her and hear her words, but I couldn't speak. I was struggling to breathe and had lost all sensation in my arms and legs, rendering them immobile. Panic set in as I felt like I was observing everything through a window—seeing and hearing it all, but unable to breathe or respond. My room was full of doctors and nurses. The environment was intense. The panic and struggle to breathe seemed to last for minutes but in reality, was a lot less time.

As I received oxygen, I slowly began to regain consciousness. Little by little, I could feel life coming back to my arms and legs. After a few minutes, I was awake and in the middle of a sense of urgency among the medical team. They swiftly brought in an X-ray machine to take images right there in my room. The X-rays revealed that I was bleeding internally. My femoral artery had been accidentally punctured and had not sealed on its own, causing internal bleeding. This internal bleeding caused my blood pressure to plummet, putting me in a life-and-death situation.

The doctors immediately contacted the University of Kentucky for consultation and considered the possibility of flying me to the UK Medical Center. It was a nightmare; I would possibly be taking my second life flight in four years. In the meantime, they had already started a bag of blood to counteract the internal bleeding, not being aware of the full extent of the bleeding. Following the consultation, the instructions were to apply pressure directly to the artery and see if the leak would seal itself, which was possible due to its location. After holding pressure on the artery, a weight was placed on the top of my thigh area where the bleeding was occurring. Within an hour, the internal bleeding had significantly slowed, and the doctors were confident that a medical flight would not be required. I was relieved but still concerned over the sense of urgency in monitoring my vitals.

Later, near supper, things were calm other than the constant monitoring of vitals. I decided I was ready to sit up and use the provided container to urinate in. As soon as I finished going to the bathroom, I started to feel nauseous, and all of a sudden my blood pressure dropped considerably, setting off a chain reaction of alarms. My breathing became difficult, and I was on the verge of passing out. This time the oxygen worked much faster, and the event was not as severe. In a few minutes, I stabilized. This event started out exactly as the one after surgery. I was never given an explanation that seemed right.

After Thursday's excitement, I was stabilized and taken out of Cardiac ICU on Friday morning. The bleeding had stopped, so I was able to be dismissed on Friday evening to go home. I was physically and emotionally drained and in a good amount of pain. I was told I could stay and go home Saturday, but I wanted to go home and escape the emotional rollercoaster. I was sick of being in a hospital.

It was nice to get home and hopefully mark the end of the crisis and the beginning of my recovery. Like a bad dream, Sunday evening, I began experiencing chest discomfort and leg pain. Concerned, I reached out to my primary care physician to see what he thought. I also reached out to my son-in-law, who is a doctor at UK Children's Hospital. Both suggested I go to the ER at UK Medical Center. At this point, I was mentally and physically exhausted, and if I needed to go to a hospital, I was ready to go to the University of Kentucky Hospital. I had been through so much over the past few weeks it was time to get a fresh set of eyes on my condition. So, on Sunday night, my wife and I started our hour and a half trip to the University of Kentucky Hospital.

Upon arrival at the University of Kentucky hospital, I was subjected to a series of tests I had previously undergone: an EKG, blood work, an echocardiogram and an ultrasound of my heart. While the results showed that my heart was functioning well, they did discover a blood clot in my leg, which had formed due to internal bleeding. This complication necessitated a new treatment plan and a change in medication. I found myself once again navigating familiar yet serious territory. It was decided that I would remain in the UK hospital for a couple more days for close monitoring with labs being drawn every four hours for two consecutive days. The blood clot was to be treated by medication, and I would have a new cardiologist in Lexington. The stay at the hospital was tiring and filled with test after test. I appreciated the thoroughness and was thankful the visit brought to light the blood clot. My condition was stable and remained so until my stay there was over.

Upon my release, the gravity of my ordeal was daunting and hard to comprehend. I was in significant discomfort due to the blood that had pooled into the soft tissue around my midsection. Every part of my body below the belt line, extending to the middle of my thighs and the insides of both legs, was a deep, bruised black. It felt as though my body had been chewed up and spit out. Part of me was amazed at what my body had been through for the past month. It all seemed like a dream.

Once home, it started to sink in that my life was going through a significant change due to a traumatic health condition. There would be medications and practices for the rest of my life due to my heart condition. I found myself in a familiar place, getting ready to begin a lengthy rehabilitation and ultimately discover my new normal. My immediate future was going to consist of doctors' visits and cardiac therapy for twelve weeks. Once again, I would be challenged with overcoming a traumatic experience. To help me mentally prepare for the difficult recovery, I thought this would be a good time to get a tattoo on my other forearm. I decided on getting the Tree of Life with the word "Strength" written above it. This most recent trauma was going to require a great deal of physical and mental strength to overcome. I was in an emotionally exhausted state and needed a reminder that I had the strength to prevail. It was a good match for the tattoo on my other forearm of "Resilient," with a picture of a bicycle.

The broken heart left me in a totally different mental state than the other traumatic experiences. In the other accidents/surgery, the damaged body would heal, and you could build muscle and strength around the affected area. Emotionally, it is hard to come to grips with the most important organ in your body being damaged. The seriousness of this was made clear on my first day of cardiac therapy. I had to have heart monitors on for my activities, which were being monitored by a nurse sitting at a computer. After every exercise, my heart rate and blood pressure were taken. All the data is recorded, as well as my "perceived effort" for each activity. Everything about the environment for cardiac therapy felt much more intense. Every time I had my vitals taken, I mentally paused and wondered if they were going to be good.

There had been a lot of fear and anxiety throughout each rehab session and during my daily life. Coming up on three months after my initial hospitalization, I still had periodic chest pains, and my body hasn't adjusted to all the new medications. Emotionally, it had been the most challenging recovery I had faced. I was focused on completing my twelve weeks of cardiac rehab. The completion would represent a milestone I would be very proud of. My other traumatic experiences helped me because I realized the emotional impact of this would last well beyond months. I had no illusions. I knew that my recovery emotionally would be a long one, and parts of this would remain with me the rest of my life. Any time I feel a pain in my chest or jaw, I will be anxious. Just today, I completed my sixteenth of thirty-six cardiac rehab sessions. Today was a difficult day because I started having chest pain while exercising. It was constant and wouldn't go away. I have not experienced chest pain during exercise that was constant. Mentally, I was angry due to the fear the pain was causing me to feel. I was so frustrated I just wanted to exercise as hard as possible, and if my heart was going to have a problem, then it could have one now. I continued exercising after I was forced to take a break until my heart rate returned to a normal range. Adapting to the emotional trauma, I am finding to be difficult. Even as I write this, hours after my session earlier today, I am still feeling periodic chest pain. After receiving stents, it is difficult to know what chest pain is normal or serious. The cardiologist informed me the body's first response is to reject the foreign items (stents). It takes months for the body to eventually accept them. It is possible to have some chest pains for months following stents being placed in your arteries.

    My broken heart issues have also brought my life value. One of the most important lessons I have learned through all my experiences is that with trauma comes gifts. This trauma has brought me the goal of completing my book. It feels like this was the event that tipped the scales for me not only to find my purpose; but act on it. I have gained confidence, empathy, thankfulness and motivation. I have learned strategies to deal with physical and emotional pain. I have also been a survivor who can share with others how to navigate trauma, deal with loss and recover from a broken heart. I would say that it is a pretty good outcome despite the tough days at rehab.

Broken Heart | 105

11
Final Thoughts & Lessons Learned

Completing my book about my traumatic experiences over the past 14 years marks a significant milestone in my life. It represents the fulfillment of a promise I made to my mother before her passing—to write a book. The purpose behind this endeavor revolves around two main reasons:

First, I aim to turn my traumatic experiences into a source of learning for others. By sharing my journey, I hope to impart the importance of resilience in overcoming trauma. Second, writing this book serves as a therapeutic process for me, aiding in my ongoing healing by allowing me to share my story with the world.

This book instills a profound sense of meaning and purpose in the traumatic events I have endured, transforming them into a beacon of hope and a guiding light for others navigating their own struggles. The journey of putting my experiences on paper and sharing them with the world has yielded numerous positive outcomes for me. Among these are the fulfillment of achieving a personal goal, the satisfaction of keeping a promise, the healing and ongoing reflection it has fostered and ultimately, the newfound purpose I have discovered in sharing my story with others.

Taking the time to reflect is an invaluable exercise for discovering one's purpose. This introspective process enables you to forge connections between your past and present, particularly in how you navigate trauma, while also illuminating your personal strengths and weaknesses. Trauma can leave both physical and emotional scars. Nevertheless, individuals have the power to choose how they will respond to these enduring reminders.

Personally, whenever I see a trigger such as a medical helicopter or an ambulance, I take a moment to express gratitude for my current health. It is also an opportunity for me to extend empathy towards those who are on their way to the hospital. This is my chosen method of responding to past trauma, rather than allowing sight and sound to trigger memories and relive the pain associated with my own helicopter and ambulance rides. I know reminders to be appreciative of your current health are valuable. Health is not a given.

Breaking free from the mindset that permits triggers to impact you is no easy feat, but it is ultimately a decision that rests with the individual. Empowering oneself to redefine responses to trauma can transform reminders of pain into moments of gratitude and compassion. Dealing with loss brought this to light for me.

The subtitle of this book, "How to Thrive, Not Just Survive," encapsulates the essence of living life on your own terms, regardless of the circumstances you face. A recurring theme throughout is the power of "individual choice." In times of trauma, it is all too easy to succumb to the role of a victim. In some ways, we are taught that misfortune creates you as a victim. It is a fact that physical and emotional pain can place a person in a position where choice feels like an unreachable option. However, as I have demonstrated, there is hope and strategies that can empower you amidst the pain.

Having a daily practice of recognizing and appreciating my current health is something I became better at after I experienced my first trauma. For instance, it is easy to think of how much you appreciate your health when you have the flu. Those who go through trauma have daily emotional and physical reminders of pain. No matter the shape you are in, on days when you are "normal," you appreciate them. I get up every day with arthritis pain in both elbow joints. Though the pain is present and uncomfortable, I appreciate my "normal." Regardless of my current physical health, I know I can feel a lot worse than my normal. My mindset has shifted to a daily positive rather than focusing on a daily negative.

Another bit of knowledge learned throughout this process is from the perspective of what the victim needs. After going through several long-term traumatic events, some of the toughest days are when you have recovered physically enough to take care of your personal needs. In my situation, this typically was when my wife went back to work. This is the time when others should reach out to those you care about. There are many days when I feel I am alone, and the emotional struggle is still there. I found that when I got a text or call from a good friend regularly, it gave me more energy and kept me in a positive frame of mind. Don't underestimate the emotional struggles after trauma. When trauma results from accidents and damage to your body, people get a false sense of healing. When someone has healed physically it doesn't mean you should stop checking in, touching base, or visiting. The emotional trauma is invisible but, in many cases, still severe. I was appreciative of my family and friends who reached out throughout my recoveries regularly. It was needed and welcomed each time.

Given the overwhelming pain associated with traumatic events, it is crucial to be proactive and plan how you wish to respond when faced with difficulty. While it is impossible to prepare for every eventuality, contemplating and planning for common challenging situations in life can be immensely beneficial. For example, the loss of a loved one is a profound experience for which one can prepare mentally and emotionally. I have discovered that making this choice can lead to personal growth opportunities. You are basically determining who you want to be in a particular situation. During loss, what kind of brother do I want to be, what kind of spouse, what kind of uncle? This type of thinking and planning moves your focus from loss, pain and grief to helping others.

Personal growth through trauma becomes an available option if you have already envisioned your desired response. For instance, losing your job can be traumatic on multiple levels. Considering how you would handle such a situation beforehand could be invaluable. Job loss can be devastating, but having a plan and developing resilience can make a significant difference. This pre-planning benefit is due to your conditioning yourself to find opportunities rather than only pain associated with trauma. The importance isn't thinking about losing your job but the practice of finding opportunities.

An age-old adage that often resonates with me, especially when navigating the aftermath of trauma, is "it could always be worse." This saying has repeatedly proven itself true throughout my life experiences.

I vividly recall my first accident back in 2010. During my initial physical therapy session, I was engulfed in misery, overwhelmed by pain and consumed by self-pity. However, my perspective shifted dramatically when I noticed someone entering the room in a wheelchair, their body visibly marked with bruises and cuts. To my surprise, I recognized the individual as he drew nearer. He was someone I knew, a former runner and cyclist who had achieved remarkable heights in his athletic career. Tragically, he had been struck by a car at an intersection, and the severity of his injuries far surpassed mine. I was further humbled to discover that the vehicle that hit him was moving at a much slower speed than the truck that collided with me. The unfortunate consequence of his severe injuries was largely due to his landing on the unforgiving pavement. In contrast, my survival and relatively lesser injuries were attributed to the fortunate circumstance of landing on a soft bed of thick grass.

Following my multilevel cervical discectomy and fusion, I found myself in a wave of pain and depression. The physical and emotional toll was immense, causing a miserable daily existence. During this time, I stumbled upon a chilling article online about someone who tragically lost his life during a cervical discectomy—a procedure that wasn't even as complex as mine. In every traumatic situation, I have witnessed someone else who was less fortunate than I. Being humbled can break you out of feeling sorry for yourself.

Time and time again, I have encountered stories on the news or in newspapers about cyclists who were fatally struck by vehicles. These grim reminders serve to underscore a harsh reality: no matter how challenging our personal struggles may seem, there is always the possibility of something far worse. This perspective, although sobering, has offered me a sense of gratitude amidst my own hardships, encouraging me to appreciate the resilience I possess in overcoming my traumatic events.

Sometimes, simple strategies are the most effective for healing after a traumatic event. Talking to someone and writing have proven to be very good ways to deal with trauma. I have used both during my struggles. Every time I speak about resilience and how it's had a positive impact on my life, I leave the venue feeling invigorated and refreshed. You don't have to go speak to a crowd about your trauma, but just talking to someone is great for healing.

Tattoos have been a godsend for me. Daily reminders on each of my forearms have been great for me. They represent survival and accomplishment. They are a reminder of the positive outcomes I have achieved despite the trauma. As I continue to go through cardiac rehabilitation, when I am working out on a few of the exercise machines, my arms are extended, and both tattoos are in view. Strength & Resilience. These serve as great motivation during my rehab. I also look at them during times when I have chest pain as positive reinforcement.

The same applies to intentionally getting out of your comfort zone and trying new things. We tend to avoid things that make us uncomfortable or that we're not very good at. I noticed that after experiencing trauma, one of the biggest changes was that things didn't appear nearly as intimidating. My perspective on life changed. Understanding you have more control over your life is empowering. Knowing you can prepare in advance for trauma and build resiliency is a powerful preparation for handling life's challenges.

I must also state that your religious beliefs can play a huge part in your recovery from trauma. I am a practicing Christian and rely a great deal on faith during traumatic events. There is a religious aspect to the traumas I have experienced. Two of the most peaceful moments of my life were during my two cycling accidents. The first conscious thoughts I had after each crash consisted of immense comfort and peace. There may be scientific explanations, but what I experienced was real and unforgettable. I have a religious aspect of my journey I plan on sharing as part of my new purpose in life.

Athletics, sports and hobbies are great resilience builders. Don't underestimate the importance of being involved as a child or adult. Conquering fears, building confidence, improving health, acquiring grit and building resilience are all benefits. I would argue that even if the only benefit was building resilience, it would be worth it. It is amazing how many potential great experiences never happen due to fear. The worst fear I have experienced is the fear of my life coming to an end. Getting the opportunity to survive makes you realize many fears are unjustified.

Trauma can and will get the individual off track from time to time. We are human and emotional beings who struggle, give in and give up at times. Recognizing this is okay, normal, but get back on track as soon as possible. I have found one of the worst negative impacts of trauma is becoming mentally and physically paralyzed. I am not referring to the permanent physical condition. I am talking about being completely overwhelmed physically and mentally. Physical or emotional pain can freeze you in place. During times like this, the goal is to move. Just keep moving when overwhelmed. Mentally and physically, you don't want to become stationary and allow the negativity and pain to keep you stuck.

Things like changing the daily routine or providing a distraction from the current circumstances can help with trauma and feeling stuck. I can remember being in the hospital and feeling miserable physically and emotionally. I needed something to change my current feelings. My solution was to take a shower. My intent was that taking a shower would break the current depressing routine. Just by taking a shower, I could change the routine and potentially feel better afterwards. Don't discount how small actions can break the paralyzed feeling of being stuck. During another hospital stay, I was physically and emotionally stuck. My solution was to put on shorts and a T-shirt and get out of the hospital gown. It was a small change, but an important change mentally.

Lastly, I believe we could do a much better job teaching and building resilience in education, at work and at home. I believe there are key times to teach resilience formally. All high school seniors and college seniors should be given lessons on resilience and how to be proactive and prepare for the challenges in life. Don't let life's challenges dictate how you react. Prepare in advance and be the person you want to be in each role/situation. Part of my purpose will be speaking to and educating these groups about the control they have in life's challenges. Individuals who struggle with trauma are another group I look forward to sharing my story with and learning from them.

Writing this book enabled me to find my purpose for this part of my life. I want this book to help others find motivation, hope, strategies and resilience to ultimately thrive in life. Thriving is so much better than surviving.

May Chapter 12 Never Come!

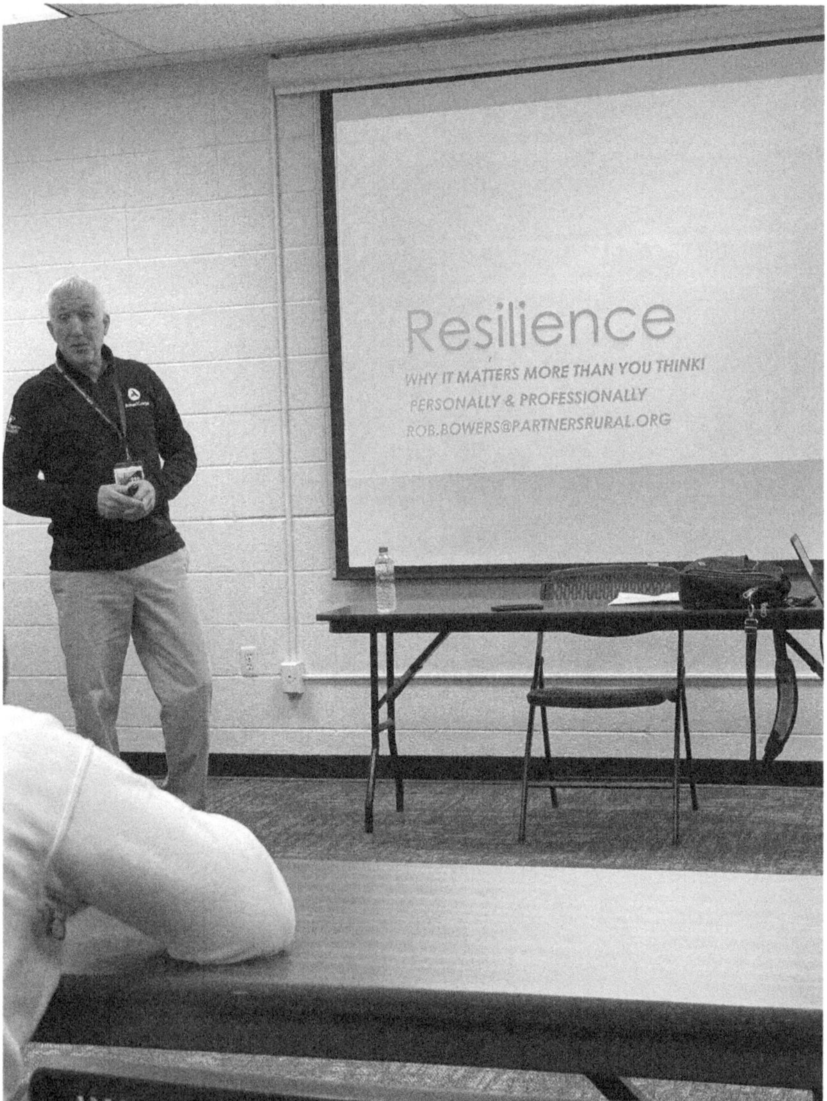
Resilience
WHY IT MATTERS MORE THAN YOU THINK!
PERSONALLY & PROFESSIONALLY
ROB.BOWERS@PARTNERSRURAL.ORG

Afterword

Over the past fourteen years I have survived two serious cycling accidents, a major surgery, helped rebuild a home after a flood, lost my mother-in-law, lost my mother and lived through a near death medical emergency.

My focus in authoring a book originally began after my second serious cycling accident. Dealing with the traumatic aftermath of two cycling accidents and a major surgery were originally going to be the focus. I had no idea how much "loss" (the deaths my mother & mother-in-law) related to trauma. Because of those losses I also gained the insight of how you can prepare for future traumatic experiences mentally and emotionally, how trauma can provide you with an opportunity for individual growth with the proper focus.

Following up the losses with a near death experience and the shock of having heart issues provided a new perspective on emotional and physical trauma. I was able to see the differences and similarities of the challenges faced recovering from each. All the traumatic events I have endured allowed me to open a new world of connecting trauma, resilience, loss and personal growth. My insight and understanding increased exponentially during the past three years.

In the end, I am grateful for the timing and blessing of surviving each experience and the unique path of discovery each has provided. My greatest satisfaction completing this book is the healing it continues to provide for me by sharing my story and future benefits with those who experience trauma.

Made in United States
Orlando, FL
30 January 2025